Understanding Judaism

UNDERSTANDING JUDAISM

by

Rabbi Daniel L. Davis

*Director, New York Federation
of Reform Synagogues*

PHILOSOPHICAL LIBRARY
New York

Printed in the United States of America

TO
SONIA

ACKNOWLEDGMENTS

To Rabbi Samuel M. Silver, Director of the Department of Public Information of the Union of American Hebrew Congregations, and to Rabbi Eugene J. Lipman, Director of the Department of Synagogue Activities of the Union of American Hebrew Congregations, for their reading of the manuscript and helpful suggestions, and to Mrs. Harry Berg for the preparation of the manuscript, I make grateful acknowledgment and express my deep appreciation.

Contents

I   Historical Outlines   1

II   Basic Concepts of Judaism   50

III   Institutions and Practices of Judaism   66

IV   The Organization of Jewish Life in America   96

V   Conversion to Judaism   102

VI   A Vocabulary of Terms of
Jewish Interest and Usage   108

VII   Reading List   113

Index   115

1 — Historical Outlines

Toward a Knowledge of Jew and Judaism

The story of the four thousand years during which Jew and Judaism grew and developed cannot and should not be told in a single volume. An encyclopedia of Jewish knowledge is needed to cover, in all the rich detail of scholarship, the history of a people, its faith and culture, language and personalities, its literature and its life. This little book seeks to indicate in barest outline some of the journeys through time of the Jewish people, touching upon some of the great spiritual destinations of Judaism, summarizing the rich achievements of thought and aspiration, and listing some of the ideas and practices responsible for a living people and its faith, a living Judaism. Only doorways to the vast vistas of Jewish history will be opened; pathways will be pointed out, that those who approach and seek a knowledge of Jew and Judaism may have guidance in the process of learning; a process, which, though it may begin with this first step, should continue through a lifetime of eager searching after knowledge and understanding.

Beginnings

Let us start with the ancient wandering tribes that found their way out of the dim, uncertain life of the nomads of the Arabian Peninsula. The Bible tells the story of these wanderers, some of whose great leaders are known to us by the names of the Patriarchs, Abraham, Isaac and Jacob, and describes them as the forbears of a people who eventually came to settle in the land of Canaan (later called

Palestine, and in part, the land called Israel on modern
maps). Some of these settlers had come from across the
Jordan River and were referred to as Ibrim—from which
the designation Hebrew derives. Others had settled in
Egypt, only to be enslaved there. With a fierce, unquench-
able desire for freedom, they broke out of Egypt, returned
to the desert, and under the leadership of Moses sought
entrance to Canaan after years of wandering.

Settlement in Canaan

In Canaan, these tribes, coming out of the desert at
various times and places, were united by the stern necessities of life in the midst of their common enemies, the
earlier settlers, who resented the newcomers. They were
involved in continuous warfare and were in constant danger of annihilation. Adapting themselves to the agricultural
life of Canaan was not easy for these nomadic tribesmen.
The temptations arising from the cults of the people of the
land were strong.

Yahveh versus Baal

Out of the desert some of these early tribes (later they
take the names that identify them as the offspring of the
Patriarch Jacob, who is called Israel—thus, the children of
Israel) brought with them the knowledge of their deity
called Yahveh. It was difficult for them to believe in their
desert deity while trying to gain a foothold and extract
a livelihood as farmers in the new land. The early Israelites
were tempted to follow the Baalim, gods of the agricultural cults, served by the people about them.

When Saul, and later David, sought to rally the people
to withstand their enemies and battle for the right to remain in the land, it is as the people of Yahveh that they
were unified. And when victory was won and their enemies
routed, the people learned that Yahveh was not without

power, even in Canaan. But it was not easy to worship Yahveh, who demanded moral conduct of the people, whose relationship to them was defined in a series of moral principles set forth in the Ten Commandments. The cults of the Baalim, developing from the primitive folk practices of an agricultural people were more easily understood and more directly related to the processes of the soil—of planting, growth and harvest. Yet, a single people emerged, and a single God, whom they were taught to serve and follow, became the unifying force. A nation was formed; a king was chosen and anointed in the name of Yahveh; a capital city, Jerusalem, was established; and a Temple built where the people came to acknowledge and to serve the one God of all the tribes.

Kings and Prophets

Saul, the first King of Israel, had united the scattered tribes into a force that had demonstrated the power of a people united. David, who followed him, was able to establish the foundations of a united people and to weld them into a nation. His successes were only partial; local jealousies and provincial interests survived despite the creation of the nation. Solomon, spared the necessity of continuous warfare against the enemies surrounding Israel, became the builder of a nation, a national polity and a national religion. In the capital city was reared the Temple, planned as the only shrine of Yahveh and where Yahveh was to be the only God of Israel. At Jerusalem a sacrificial cult was established, the worship of Yahveh was purified and placed on a higher plane than that of the local shrines, where the Canaanitish Baal cults exercised their influence. Israel began to be a nation, the religion of Israel began to develop from a tribal cult to the religion of a people. In this sense Judaism may be described as the religion of the Jewish people.

Great personalities, like Abraham, certainly glimpsed

the first vision of the nature of God. Abraham became the
father of a people dedicated to the search for the true
understanding and service of God. Moses was a liberator
of a people from even more than physical bondage. He
brought them to the revelation at Sinai where they might
share in the process of discovering the meaning of spiritual
freedom. The moral basis upon which this new faith of a
primitive people was to be built was the result of the efforts
of a countless number of teachers, men of genius who
pondered the great problems of man's relation to God and
taught the people that God was no mere desert deity,
no local Baal, whose fierce and frightening image was often
served by the most degrading practices. These geniuses of
the spirit, most of them unknown, many of them referred
to as the prophets of Israel, represented a unique phe-
nomenon in history. They were not priests of a shrine, they
did not minister at the sacrificial altar of the Temple, they
did not belong to any one part of the people. They spoke
to kings and people alike, often rebuking both for failing
to appreciate the moral imperatives of the religion of
Israel. Out of their teaching, more than from the military
conquests of the kings, came the unifying power that was
to make Israel a people and Yahveh—God.

*Kingdoms Come and Go—The Word of the Lord
Remaineth*

Whatever was the political skill of a Solomon in uniting
a people, it possessed little lasting power to hold them
together. The tribes united as a people did not survive
the death of Solomon. They were divided into two kingdoms, Israel or Samaria as the northern ten tribes came
to be called, and Judah or Judea, the southern kingdom,
composed of the tribes of Judah and Benjamin. A series
of kings ruled Samaria with no distinction, except that one
seemed to be worse than the other. Caught between Assyria

to the north and Egypt to the south, the northern Kingdom of Israel came to an end in 719 B.C.E. Its people were carried off captive to Assyria. Assyrians were brought to settle in the land of Israel. What happened to the Ten Tribes? They disappeared, assimilated among the lost peoples of the Middle East, with only the Biblical stories as their history and memorial.

Judah survived as a very little nation. Perhaps its smallness was the key to its survival. It constituted no threat to the powers that surrounded it, struggling with one another for domination. With the example of Samaria's fate before them, the people of Judah were more inclined to pay attention to the prophets. Perhaps these teachers of religion knew what they were talking about—that the failure to create a moral society had resulted in the dissolution of a kingdom; that the neglect of God's law of justice was followed by the natural consequences of suffering, for the individual and for the nation; that religion was more than the cult of the sacrificial altar. Even as Amos had spoken, "Hate the evil, and love the good, and establish justice in the gate; it may be that the Lord, the God of hosts, will be gracious unto the remnant of Joseph." In little Judah it would seem that the impact of these words was felt, and during the reign of Hezekiah, it appeared as if the dawn of a new and better age had come. It was a time when the prophet's words were heard. King and people seemed to hearken. "Behold, a king shall reign in righteousness. And as for princes, they shall rule in justice. . . .The vile person shall be no more called liberal, nor the churl said to be noble. . . . And the work of righteousness shall be peace and the effect of righteousness quietness and confidence forever." (Is. 32:1,17) Although the prophet had spoken often the words of warning and chastisement, he had also offered the way of hope, and counseled the power that man possesses to find redemption from sin and recovery from the consequences of his failure to follow after righteousness.

"A remnant shall return, even the remnant of Jacob unto God, the Mighty. . . ." (Is. 10:21)

The events of the times had prompted the prophet to warn of doom and destruction. The concept of God, as a God of justice, a God of love and of mercy, to be served only by men of moral purpose described in Micah's words—

> And what doth the Lord require of thee:
> Only to do justly, and to love mercy, and to walk
> humbly with thy God. (Micah 6:8)

provides the basis for forgiveness and redemption:

> Who is a God like unto Thee, that
> pardoneth the iniquity,
> And passeth by the transgression
> of the remnant of His heritage?
> He retaineth not His anger for ever,
> Because He delighteth in mercy. (Micah 7:18)

Ethical Monotheism

Again, under King Josiah, another period of revival and reform set in, encouraged by the prophet Jeremiah. In this time a great document was discovered while repairs were being made to the Temple: the book of Deuteronomy, a portion of Scriptures bearing the imprint of the prophetic spirit. In this book, called "repetition of the law," is set forth a clear description of Judaism as ethical monotheism. The Shema, which came to be the central affirmation of the faith of the Jew, "Hear, O Israel, the Lord our God, the Lord is One" (Dt. 6:4), appears for the first time, giving expression to the absolute unity of God. This is followed by the call to "love the Lord thy God with all thy heart . . ." and an injunction to reject every form of idolatry.

The people of Israel, described in Deuteronomy as a

"holy people," are commanded to fulfill their holiness by carrying out the moral injunctions set before them. Not only the Ten Commandments are found in Deuteronomy, but laws for the regulation of national and individual life; laws concerning family life, agricultural practices, treatment of the poor, the stranger, the worker, the sick. The weak and the helpless are not overlooked in the book, whose style and thought bear marked resemblance to that of prophetic utterance. With Deuteronomy, the prophets, the teachers of Israel had succeeded in formulating a religion marked by the great ideals and concepts that were to raise Judaism from provincial cult to world faith, and Israel from a tribal grouping to a people dedicated to the service of God, to the transmitting and teaching of His moral law to the nations of the earth.

Prey to Power

Before Josiah died, the struggle for world power between Egypt to the south of Judah and Babylonia to the north began again. Judah fell under the sway of Egypt, only to be laid under siege by Nebuchadnezzar of Babylonia. In 586 B.C.E. the people of Judah were carried off captive to Babylonia, their capital city, Jerusalem, left in ruins, the Temple destroyed, and it would seem that the end had come for Judah.

The Babylonian exile did not swallow up the people of Judah by the process of assimilation. In exile the people learned the validity of the prophetic teachings. What had happened to them was not because their God was too weak to support them or bring them victory in battle. God was strong enough even to use great nations to do His will that people might learn the consequences of failing to carry out His law.

O Asshur, the rod of Mine anger . . .
I do send him against an ungodly nation . . .(Is. 10:5,6)

The prophet had taught that God was the God of all people. As He was one, His law was one for all mankind. Their suffering had come not because God had forsaken them, but to teach them to return to God and experience the redemptive love of His goodness.

Take unto you words,
And return unto the Lord;
Say unto Him: Forgive all iniquity,
And accept that which is good . . . (Hos. 14:3)

I will heal their backsliding,
I will love them freely . . . (Hos. 14:5)

Lessons and Achievements in Exile

In exile the people of Judah learned the validity of what the prophets had taught. This gave them hope and purpose. In their deeply felt need they came together to voice their aspiration, to learn from one another the meaning of what the prophets had taught, and to help and strengthen one another. Out of this threefold and natural need of a people to preserve their spiritual integrity was born the Synagogue, as place of prayer, as place of learning, as place of fellowship, where men may turn for help to their brothers. Perhaps the oldest term for Synagogue is Bes Am—"House of the People." It was this house, established out of their need, that was to serve them in exile, and be with them as a spiritual center through the long ages of their existence.

The conquest of Babylonia by Cyrus, King of Persia, brought near the realization of the hope of the captive people. The words of the prophet now began to ring true not only with comfort but with fulfillment:

Comfort ye, comfort ye My people
Saith your God.

Bid Jerusalem take heart,
And proclaim unto her,
That her time of service is accomplished . . .(Is. 40:1,2)

Return and Restoration

In 538 B.C.E. Cyrus permitted the captive Judeans to return to their land. They set themselves to the task of rebuilding the country, to re-establishing the Temple, to gathering together the materials out of which a people's life might be constituted, and in collecting the scattered, but not forgotten Scriptures that contained the law by which a people might live. The people that had remained in the land, the Samaritans, a mixture of old settlers and those that had been settled there as occupying forces by conquering nations, sought to interfere with the work of restoring the land and the Temple. From Persia came Ezra and Nehemiah with the full support of the Persian King to aid the people of Judah in the tasks of rebuilding.

Seeing the danger of assimilation, Ezra proposed that the people refuse to intermarry with the foreign peoples in the land, so that the small and reconstituted community of Judah (now referred to as Judea) might not lose its spiritual integrity as the holy people of the Lord. Ezra then began the work of teaching the people the Law of the Lord, of gathering the Scriptures that were to be their guide, the constitution of their reconstituted life as the Jewish people. The Torah, or Law, thus came to have a very real meaning for these people who felt a need to live by the mandates of God's Law.

For two centuries the people of Judea lived the simple, peaceful life of a theocracy, turning to their teachers (the Soferim, those who had written down the words of the prophets and sages) for guidance, consulting them about the Law for the knowledge of God's ways. In this period, living necessity was the design that gave form to the Scriptures of the Jewish people, so that their Bible, in time to become the Bible of a large part of the world, developed out of the life of a people who chose to be ruled by God, and thus became the people of God.

Contact with Hellenism

Judea did not attempt to resist Alexander the Great as he spread the rule of Greece in his conquest of the world. When his generals divided his empire, Judea fell under the dominion of the Ptolemies. In and out of Egypt, Greek culture spread, and its influence was felt in Judea. Greek terms found their way into Jewish usage; Greek thought and communities of Greek-speaking Jews influenced one another. There had been an Aramaic translation of the Bible for those who spoke the dialect brought from Babylonia. Now the need for a Greek translation began to be felt by the Greek-speaking communities such as that of Alexandria, so that they might have recourse to the Books of the Law, and the Prophets and the Holy Writings. It is intriguing to speculate on what might have resulted from this cultural contact between Hellenism and Judaism had it been permitted to develop. However, when the Seleucid Kings gained domination over Judea, this placid state of affairs was not allowed to continue.

Struggle for Freedom of the Spirit

Greek culture became an instrument of political conquest in the hands of Antiochus Epiphanes, who, seeking to impose Hellenism upon the people of Judea, turned the Temple at Jerusalem into a shrine for the Olympian Zeus. This stirred the little band of unmilitary people to revolt, and a war for religious liberty began, led by Judah Maccabeus. The victory won in this war (165 B.C.E.) is celebrated in the Chanukah Festival, the Feast of Dedication, marking the recovery of the Temple and its restoration to the worship of God. The family of the Maccabeans, known as Hasmoneans, did not stop with attainment of religious liberty. They were bent also on securing political independence for Judea, and they established themselves as a dynasty.

The Hasmoneans were the last group of rulers over Judea. The independent kingdom did not long remain independent. Alliance with Rome was followed by Judea becoming in the end a procuratorship of the Roman Empire.

Sects and Parties—Conquest and Exile Again

The last century of Judea as a political entity was marked by unrest and confusion, and, strangely enough, the development of the spiritual elements by which Jew and Judaism were to be enabled to live in the world. The end of the national existence of Judea was to be followed by the world career of the Jew. Before the end there arose a number of parties in Judea, each representing a different approach to the problem of survival. Those who believed in political power, the Sadducees, were supporters of the king and ruling class. Religiously they subscribed solely to the authority of Scripture, insisted on a strict interpretation of the Torah, believing that the rule of the people should rest in the hands of the priesthood and the aristocracy.

The Pharisees were the party of the people, to whom they taught the meaning and power of the Law, not a law limited to the written word, but one whose principles and spirit might be applied, through study and interpretation, to every relationship and need of life. The Pharisees did not put their trust in kings and rulers; they feared the corruption bred by empire. They preferred to find their strength in following the Law of God that had sustained them with a knowledge of the right and the good in all times and under all the changing circumstances of life.

As the conditions of life grew worse, as the rulers became more corrupt and the power of Rome more oppressive and exacting, other parties came into being. The Essenes turned in flight from the intolerable conditions brought about by corruption and oppression. They formed themselves into communities to follow the simple life, sharing all the work of their hands and the produce of their toil.

Others took an opposite approach; the Zealots urged an activist opposition to their oppressors and sought to stir the people to revolt. And among the people there were those who put their hope in the coming of a Messiah, the God-sent leader who would redeem them from their woes, re-establish the rule of righteousness under God's law and usher in the age of peace and prosperity.

Of these parties, only the Pharisees had a lasting influence upon the future of the people and their survival as an organized community in the world. The Zealots did succeed in stirring the people to revolt, which brought upon them the crushing might of Rome; the siege of Jerusalem and the destruction of the city and the second Temple in the year 70 C.E. Thousands were sold into slavery, hundreds of the leaders carried off to Rome to march in the triumphal procession of Vespasian and Titus. The Sadducees ceased to exist as the aristocracy and the priesthood were scattered. Those who looked for a Messiah had come to believe that Jesus of Nazareth had appeared in order to fill that role, and through him they would find their redemption. They formed a new sect, the Redeemed or Christians, and later, under the leadership of Saul of Tarsus, founded the movement that was to bring Christianity to the world. Many of the poor and the peasants and their teachers remained in the land, as Jews did throughout the centuries, refusing to abandon the place which had given birth to them as a people and to their faith.

New Designs of Jewish Life—From Little Nation to Widespread Influence in the World

Rome had destroyed Judea as a nation. As a people the Judeans or Jews continued to seek their spiritual destiny

—and in many ways were to increase their influence in the world. In Javneh or Javnia, Jochanan ben Zakkai established an academy to foster Jewish learning. From this academy scholars were to go forth to teach the Jew the meaning of Judaism, the application of the Torah as a law for the guidance and ennoblement of life. The Synagogue became the mobile center of Jewish life. It depended on no central or single Temple at Jerusalem. Wherever the Jew lived, his Synagogue as place of prayer and learning and social helpfulness was reared and served to give meaning and form to his life. As the diaspora, or scattered communities of Jewish life, came into being with Jews living in every center of population of the ancient world, a new design of Jewish life was in the process of formation. In Babylonia academies were established where the Torah was studied and taught. Sura and Pumbeditha, Nehardea and Machuza became centers to which large numbers of the people were attracted. Jewish learning was not limited to the scholars. The Kallah, a periodic institute for popular adult studies, brought thousands of the common people to these centers of learning to be instructed in the law of Jewish life.

Torah—The Law of Life

The Torah had come to include a vast store of teachings based upon the written word. In time the teachings of the Tannaim (scholars or rabbis who interpreted the Law) had become too extensive for oral transmission. The rabbis set themselves to the task of creating a textbook of the oral Law. Jehudah ha-Nasi, Judah the Prince, was the compiler of a standard collection which came to be known as the Mishnah. The same process of teaching and interpretation was continued in the effort to keep the Law as the living word for the guidance of the people. Later generations of rabbis, called the Amoraim, added their interpretations to the Mishnah. In time the Mishnah and Gemarah, as the later interpretations were called, were compiled into

great collections known as the Talmud. Out of the Babylonian and Palestinian centers of learning emerged these
encyclopedias of Jewish teaching for the guidance of the
people.

Thus a unique kind of community life was created by
the Jews in the centuries that followed the dispersion from
ancient Judea. This life lacked political organization, yet
it had the true and lasting integrity of a people dedicated
to the service of God and to living by His Law. The people
were self-ruled. Education was necessary so that all might
know the Law and be able to live by it. The center of their
life was the Synagogue, the symbol of their culture the
school, the source of their strength the home. Their social
responsibilities were expressed in charity, in institutions of
help and hospitality for the poor, the dependent and the
stranger.

The Unconquerable Spirit

It was not surprising that, in a period when Rome had
conquered Judea, the Jewish spirit was not crushed, and
many people were attracted to Judaism as a way of life
that gave meaning and value to human existence. Graetz,
in his *History of the Jews*, makes frequent reference to
those who became converts to Judaism, and characterizes
this tendency by writing: "It is an extraordinary fact that
during the half century after the destruction of the Jewish
State, there were everywhere conversions to Judaism, both
in the East and in Asia Minor, but especially in Rome."
(Volume II, page 383.) Later, when Christianity became
the official religion of Rome, and in the period when Islam
sought to conquer the world for Mohammedanism, conversions to Judaism were interdicted by the ruling powers.
Yet, Judaism did not cease to be a world religion, for
wherever Jews lived, the Jewish community, the Synagogue, Jewish life, were the visible symbols of a vital faith.

Among Arab Peoples—Mohammedanism Is Born

Jews settled in every part of the known world of ancient times. As the Babylonian communities declined, Jews
had already established themselves in Arab lands and in
the North African countries. From the Jews of Arabia,
Mohammed derived many of the ideas that he made basic
to his own new found faith: the concept of the one God,
of man's duty, the importance of prayer and charity. But
when the Jewish communities refused to follow Mohammed
or to regard him as the true prophet of the Lord, Mohammed, once their friend and disciple of their spirit,
turned against them. Despite the fact that Islam soon conquered all the lands of Asia Minor and of North Africa,
Jews continued to live and even to flourish in the Moslem
empire. In some instances the coming of the Moslem con-
querors relieved Jewish communities of the more oppressive measures of Christian rulers. As Moslem rule spread,
elements of Arabic culture were carried with it and had
a beneficent influence upon Jewish life and thought.

East and West—Linked by Scholars

During the period of Mohammedan rise to power, the
Jewish communities of Babylon experienced a revival,
with the Exilarch restored as the head of the Jewish community. The academies of Babylon likewise entered upon
a new period of activity. Their heads, called the Gaon of
Sura or the Gaon of Pumbeditha, were regarded as the
spiritual leaders of the Jewish communities. Their pre-
eminence as teachers was recognized not only in Babylon,
but by communities in North Africa, in Spain, and even
in France, and many inquiries dealing with religious matters were addressed to them. The inquiries and their an-
swers came to constitute a whole body of literature, based

upon the Talmud, but representing the opinions of scholars who were concerned with the needs and developing conditions of life and its problems. In time scholars were sent from the centers of learning to distant communities, to convey instruction and to secure contributions for the support of the academies, thus unifying the life and culture of the Jews, despite their scattered existence in the far-flung communities of many lands.

Influence of Mohammedan World

Mohammedan culture had other influences on Jewish life: the Jews developed an interest in poetry and grammar, philosophy and mathematics. The poetry, as Jews wrote it, was sacred poetry and became part of the prayerbook. Grammatical studies led to the vocalizing of the text of the Bible, so that several generations of Bible students, known as Massoretes (whose work began before the Islamic period), were able to produce a fixed and reliable text of the Bible.

This interest in Bible studies was responsible for a movement of reaction begun in the eighth century against rabbinical interpretation of Scriptures. A group known as Karaites, scripturalists, arose who rejected the teachings of the rabbis, seeking all direction for Jewish life from the Bible alone. While Karaism continued for several centuries, it did not have a permanent place in Jewish life. Its spirit was contrary to the needs of life, which require constant and changing interpretation of the Torah, else it ceases to have influence and meaning. One of the great scholars of the time, Saadia Gaon, in his writings, which include a philosophical treatise, *Emunos ve-Deos* (*Beliefs and Opinions*), expressed his opposition to Karaism.

Aware of the needs of Jews living in the Arab world, Saadia translated the Bible into Arabic, and wrote commentaries in Arabic. Born in Egypt, Saadia went to Palestine and ultimately to Babylon, where he became the Gaon of

Sura. In the wide range of his thought and writing, Saadia was an exemplar of the scholar-leader of Jewish life who flourished during the Moslem period.

Westward Movement

In time the great centers of Jewish life moved westward along the shores of the Mediterranean. Communities in North Africa and Spain came into being as those in Babylonia began to decline. Asia Minor became the bridge over which Jews traveled to many distant parts of the world. By the end of the tenth century Jews were settled in India and Russia, in Spain and France, and had penetrated as far as China. There is an account of a whole people, the Khazars, who lived in the land between the Black and Caspian seas, who voluntarily accepted Judaism under the leadership of their King, Bulan, and were known as a Jewish Kingdom until destroyed by the Tartar invasion in the middle of the thirteenth century. In all these lands communities were established in which the same pattern of organized Jewish life prevailed. Every Jew was part of the community, Jews were governed by the rule of the Torah, scholars were their leaders, Synagogue and school were the central institutions of their life. Jews moved about in the ancient world, traveling from Rome to Toledo, from Cairo to Cologne, from India to China, bearing the culture of Jewish learning. Everywhere the Jews were under the rule of a political order in which they were not permitted to share, and were subjected to harsh decrees and exactions. But in spite of all hardships, the Jewish community maintained itself as a religious community, characterized by a love of learning and piety, and a sense of social responsibility which extended even to distant communities, sharing their faith and destiny as the people of God.

Golden Age in Spain

In the eighth century the Mohammedans conquered the
Visigoth rulers of Spain. Jews who had fled from the persecutions of the Visigoths returned to Spain where they
established and continued for five centuries what has been
described as the "Golden Age" of Jewish life. Jews were
able to acquire estates and live on the land. Others became
merchants and traveled to distant lands as they encouraged
international commerce. Hasdai ibn Shaprut, physician to
the khalif, became his diplomatic representative and was
instrumental in making treaties of peace with the Christian
kings. A Samuel ibn Naghdela started as a grocer, but his
learning in the fields of philosophy, language and mathematics won him the position as secretary to the Grand
Vizier of Malaga, adviser to the King of Granada, and
Nagid or head of the Jewish community. Solomon ibn Gabirol, Moses ibn Ezra, and Jehuda ha-Levi were the poet-
philosophers of the eleventh and twelfth centuries, whose
magnificent works in Hebrew have been preserved, some
becoming the poetry of the people by inclusion in the
prayer book. Abraham ibn Ezra wrote commentaries on
the Bible, and Benjamin of Tudela recorded his experiences
and observations during his travels extending over thirteen
years. Bachya ibn Pakuda, a judge in his community in the
twelfth century, wrote a philosophical work, *Duties of the
Heart,* which has been read and studied by Jews everywhere through the centuries down to our own.

The greatness of this period of intellectual genius in
Jewish life is most nobly illustrated in the life and work
of Moses Maimonides, born in Cordova in 1135. Forced
to leave Spain while still a youth, Maimonides fled with
his father to North Africa, later sought to settle in Palestine,
where the disorders created by the Crusades made his
return to Egypt necessary. As a physician, Maimonides

gained fame which led to his appointment in that capacity to the Sultan Saladin and his court. He was a great physician, and some of his medical writings are read with admiration even today. The breadth and understanding of his medical knowledge alone would have earned him an important place in history. Maimonides was at home in every branch of science and thought. His great philosophical work, *Moreh Nebuchim* (*The Guide of the Perplexed*), in which he seeks a reconciliation of reason and faith, demonstrates the reasonableness of Judaism. In his *Mishneh Torah* or *Yad ha-Chazakah* (*The Mighty Hand*), he organized and systematized the mass of material in Mishnah and Talmud and later commentaries, providing in lucid Hebrew a guide to the Torah which can be easily read and understood. His Thirteen Principles, stating the basic beliefs of Judaism, found their way into the prayer book, and became the text of sacred hymns, such as the Yigdal. Maimonides wrote with facility in both Hebrew and Arabic, on history and mathematics, astronomy and natural science. His writings were frequently consulted by medieval Christian Scholastics, who, because of their references to these works, helped preserve them.

Crusades and Martyrdom

Outside of Spain there was no "Golden Age." The Crusades, inaugurated by the Popes to reclaim the "Holy Land" from the Moslems, "infidels" and "Moors" as they were variously called, sent bands of men and even children on the march to Palestine. On the way, the Crusaders became marauding bands, attacking, looting and destroying Jewish communities, particularly those along the Rhine. In France and Germany, from the eleventh to the thirteenth century, thousands of Jews died the martyr's death at the hands of those, who, aroused by the appeal of religion, committed the most bestial and irreligious acts. How the Jews sur-

vived this period of terror is difficult to explain, except in
terms of the spirit, which has a heroism that triumphs over
the most terrible cruelties, that lives despite the most
crushing blows.

In Germany, France and England, the Jews who survived the Crusades, became the victims of their rulers, who
regarded the Jew as their property, subject to their whims
and rapacious desires. Without protest their goods were
seized, their property taxed and even their dead held for
ransom. When Rabbi Meir of Rothenburg tried to leave the
city, he was seized and imprisoned. Rudolph of Hapsburg
refused twenty thousand marks offered for his release. It
was not enough. When Meir of Rothenburg died, it took
fourteen years for the Jews to reclaim his body for Jewish
burial.

Attacked by Fire, Falsehood and Torture

Everywhere the Church sought to win the Jew to
Christianity. No method to achieve this end—persecution,
exile, confiscation of property, disputations and false
charges—was barred. Where the word did not succeed,
the sword was tried; where persuasion failed, torture was
employed. The Jew became a strange and fearful legend,
at times accused of ritual murder even though Popes and
rulers declared them innocent of the charge. At times Jews
were charged with "desecrating the host"—the communion
wafer—and at other times the Talmud was placed on trial
and Jews were called upon to defend the work. But the
Talmud was found guilty and burned at the stake, unless
a sufficiently large bribe could be raised to save the precious volumes from destruction.

In Spain, as the Christian rulers replaced the Mohammedan, the Inquisition was used by the clergy, with the
help of the kings, to convert the Jews to Christianity. Many
Jews were won to the Church. They could not live other-

wise, their lives and their property were in danger, and often, even after conversion, accused of secretly relapsing back into Judaism, the converts were tortured and their property confiscated. In Spain, Marrano was the name given to a "secret Jew," who publicly professed a belief in Christianity, but secretly practiced Judaism. The Inquisition sought out the Marranos with every device of spying, denunciation and torture. Hundreds were found out, arrested and burned at the stake, hundreds more fled for their lives to lands beyond the reach of the Inquisition.

As this reign of terror spread over Europe its pall of burnings at the stake, expulsions and confiscations, it was not difficult to understand why conversion became abhorrent to the Jew, and proselytes were not sought or even encouraged. Too many Jews became converts under duress, too many Jews paid the toll of their very lives in refusing to convert, for Jews to regard the conversion process with anything but aversion and disgust. Yet, there were Christians, who, recognizing the spiritual values in Judaism, became willing converts to it even during the dark centuries of Jewish persecutions. And many Jews, once out of the range of persecution, discarded the Christianity they had been forced to accept and returned to Judaism.

Expulsion from Spain

The Inquisition failed to convert all the Jews of Spain, or even to keep as Christians all those Jews whom it had forced to be converted. In 1492 King Ferdinand of Spain issued the edict of expulsion of the Jews. By August 2 of that year the last of the Jews had left Spain. Some died on the way to lands of refuge, others for a short while found uneasy asylum in Portugal, from which they were ordered expelled in 1496. Columbus, bound on his great voyage of discovery, and some say financed by the confiscated funds of the Jews, and with a crew in part recruited from Mar-

ranos, who thus found a means of escape from their tor-
turers, wrote in his ship's log that he passed the ships that
were carrying the last Jews away from Spain.

Haven and Survival

The fifteenth century closed with the tragic dissolution
of a community of more than a quarter of a million Jews,
who for five centuries had created a rich culture of learning
and life, and had contributed to the commerce and industry of the Spanish people. It is not difficult to explain
the decline of Spain, that had thus drained itself of so much
of the lifeblood of its culture and economy. The decline
of Spain was of little comfort to the wandering refugees,
who sought a resting place where they might rebuild their
lives. Some of them found new homes in Turkey and the
Isles of Greece of the Ottoman Empire; others made their
way to Holland. The Dutch, at that time at war with
Spain, and antagonistic toward the Papists, thus were tol-
erant toward the Jews, victims of the persecution of the
Catholic kings.

The Spanish Jews carried little with them except their
faith, their learning and language, the baggage of the
spirit that is not easily lost or stolen. They preserved the
Sephardic tradition as it was called, the Spanish forms
of worship. They still spoke among themselves a language,
Hispaniolish or Ladino, part Spanish, part Hebrew. They
retained their sense of dignity as individuals, and love of
learning as a people. Strangely enough, their spiritual re-
sources, the study of the Torah, helped to inspire Christian
scholars in the study of the Bible, and the study of medicine
helped to bring healing and hope to many who had sought
to destroy the Jew. The Jew became the true exponent of
the doctrine of "returning good for evil."

England

Jews had settled in England by the tenth century, and were found in great numbers in London in the time of William the Conqueror. For a century they lived more or less at peace in England. With the reign of King Richard the Lion-Hearted and his departure for a crusade, riots broke out that resulted in the massacre of many Jews, and the suicide of others, who took their own lives rather than fall into the hands of the mob. Caught between the clergy that sought to convert them and thus rob them of the faith of their fathers, and the rulers who stripped them of their property to the point where they could no longer maintain their existence, the Jews found in the edict of expulsion in 1290 at least a way out. In that year some sixteen thousand Jews left England.

Some Effects of Suffering

How did the Jew react to these terrible experiences? What happened to the spirit of the Jew, so sorely tried by exile and exactions, beset for centuries by the wild dogs that preyed upon him, seeking to snatch both faith and fortune from him?

The Jew turned his thoughts inward and upward. Many sought to find the hidden promises of redemption in the study of the Bible and Talmud, and assigned mystical meaning to what seemed to be the simple expressions of their Scriptures. Their thoughts ranged through metaphysical speculations as they sought new explanations for the nature of God, His relationship to the world, to Israel and to mankind. These studies known as Cabbalah, or Tradition, created a vast literature of mystical interpretation. Most notable in this literature was the Zohar, which appeared in thirteenth-century Spain, a commentary on the Pentateuch ascribed to Simon ben Yohai, who had lived in the

second century. In the East, Isaac Luria, who taught in
Safed, Palestine in the sixteenth century, was one of the
great personalities among the Cabbalists gathered there.
The Cabbalah represented a flight from rationalism to the
shadowy realms, where the spirit sought to fathom the
meaning of the Divine plan.

This sort of intense speculation on the nature of God,
this probing for hidden meanings led many to look for
indications of the coming of the Messiah, the supernatural
messenger of God, who would redeem his people from woe
and oppression. This hope for the Messiah was as old as
the words of Isaiah:

> And there shall come forth
> a shoot out of the stock of Jesse . . .
> And the spirit of the Lord
> shall rest upon him . . .
> With righteousness shall he judge
> the poor, and decide with equity
> for the meek of the land—
> And the wolf shall dwell with the lamb . . .
> For the earth shall be full of the
> knowledge of the Lord. (11:1-9)

Hope for a Redeemer

The eager, trusting spirit of the Jew was never turned
to bitterness and hatred. The hope for the Messiah sustained him with the abiding thought that God in His own
good time and way would send one to redeem His people
from the evils that afflicted them. The greater the evils,
the deeper became the yearning of the people for a redeemer, until, even as the mirage suggests an oasis to the
thirsty wanderer in the desert, the unreal appeared to take
form. Thus, there arose messiahs, or those who were
claimed to be such, and the weary, but hopeful spirit of
many Jews believed, and followed after the mirage. David

Reubeni, David Molcho, Sabbathai Zevi and Jacob Frank were the names of those who appeared as a cloud of hope and disappeared in the winds of disillusion.

Places of Refuge

Some Jews, after years of wanderings, found places where they were welcome, and could live for a while in peace. In Italy, the Popes often gave refuge to the Jews. Jewish physicians looked after the health of the Popes. Jewish scholars, like Obadiah Sforno and Elias Levita, taught Christian scholars, who sought in Hebrew learning to advance their own comprehension of the Scriptures. Among Jewish scholars who flourished in Italy were Elias de Medigo and Judah Messer Leon, philosophers; Joseph Ha Cohen, who wrote the *Vale of Tears*, a historical account of Jewish sufferings in the Middle Ages; Azariah dei Rossi, who wrote on history and literature in his *Enlightenment of the Eyes*.

In Turkey many Spanish Jews found refuge. Among them was Joseph Caro, the author of the *Shulchan Aruch (Prepared Table)*, the guide to Jewish law and practice, still consulted by the Orthodox of our own day. Others, like Don Joseph Nasi, who became the Duke of Naxos, settled in Constantinople and there became adviser to the Sultan. His aunt, Donna Grazia Mendesia, became a great lady, whose philanthropies and encouragement of culture and learning won her a reputation as a Jewish noble-woman in the twelfth century.

In Poland Jews found a welcome as the necessary middle class in a population made up of serfs and nobles. In Polish lands, which included Polish Russia or Ruthenia and Lithuania, Jews were able to organize themselves into communities and even a council of communities, as the Vaad Arba Aratzoth, the Council of Four Lands, might be described. The Vaad brought Jews together in semi-annual sessions to discuss matters of mutual concern and welfare.

The Council also appointed a *shtadlan,* an official ambassador of the Jews, who called at the Polish court and sought to influence the Polish kings so that no harsh measures would be taken against the Jews.

Eastern Europe—Light and Shadow

As conditions in Eastern Europe were better than in Western Europe, Jews migrated from the Germanic lands. With them they brought the German tongue that they had been accustomed to use. Thus German, to which Slavic words were added as Jews settled in the Polish lands, became Judeo-German, or Jüddish, or Yiddish, the added language of Jews in a great part of Europe. Jews wrote in Yiddish and created a vast Yiddish literature, which included one of the most popular works, an ethical commentary on the Five Books of Moses, the *Tze-enah u-Re'enah,* read by Jewish women in the Synagogue.

In 1648, a Cossack uprising led by Bogdan Chmielnicki, swept over Poland, destroying Jews and Poles, sparing only those who accepted Greek Orthodoxy. The uprising was followed by Russia going to war with Poland, and the Russian invaders wiped out the Jews who had escaped Chmielnicki. It is estimated that as many as a half-million Jews lost their lives as victims of Cossack uprisings and Russian wars, and the darkness of great suffering and despair settled over all of Eastern Europe at the opening of the eighteenth century.

But the Spirit Has Its Own Power

Both Jews and Jewish life were engaged in a struggle for survival. On every side restrictive laws prevented Jews from engaging in the normal pursuits of artisan and farmer. Widespread poverty made the lot of the Jew a hard one to bear. Added to this were the charges of the clergy, who sought to destroy Judaism by arousing the non-Jewish populace to acts of violence against the Jews. Surrounded by suspicion, repressed by economic restrictions, denied the opportunities of freedom and citizenship, their very lives frequently in jeopardy, for the Jews, the Jewish community became more than the enforced Jewish quarter or ghetto. It was a spiritual haven, where study of the Torah, where the concern of Jew for fellow Jew, where the inwardness of Jewish life provided the saving grace of courage and dignity and faith in the future. Poor and harassed as many Jews in Eastern Europe were, it was not always possible for them to do more than snatch a few moments at the end of the day to review a Psalm or to listen on a Sabbath afternoon to a homily on a verse from Scriptures. Even then, through the darkened spirit and troubled mind, the light of learning found its way with difficulty.

As in centuries before, the Cabbalah spoke to the inner need and yearning of the people, so in the eighteenth century, Chassidism provided an answer to the emotional hunger of the Jew. Israel ben Eliezer of Podolia, an orphan lad, and later teacher of little children, eager to live more closely to nature, went into the Carpathian mountains to earn a livelihood as a limedigger. He spent much of his time in contemplation and in the study of mystical literature. From his knowledge of plants and herbs gained in the woods, he made healing preparations for the poor, who sought him out. With his herbs he gave a kind word, a prayer, a moral tale, advice and hopeful guidance. The people were drawn to this pious man, whose sense of faith and powers of understanding were as a balm to their own troubled lives. They called him Israel Baal Shem Tov— Israel, Master of the Good Name—abbreviated as Besht. The Besht did not teach the people with learned and involved disquisitions; but by simple tales he conveyed to them great truths and helped them reach out for a knowledge of God. He taught Judaism of the heart, the joy to be found in prayer, the greatness of simple acts of goodness, the power that every man has in his own soul to find God.

His teachings were passed on from person to person, from
community to community. Others who caught his spirit
began to teach in his fashion. His followers soon gathered
other groups about them and they called their teacher the
Zaddik, "the righteous one." The followers of the Zaddikim
were in turn known as the Chassidim, "the pious ones."
Within a generation there swept over southeastern Europe
this pietistic movement, Chassidism, with its appeal to the
emotions, its emphasis upon the simple virtues, its use of
folk song and spontaneous dances, of story and parable, as
the means of leading the people to God and to finding joy
in His service. This was one of the ways in which the faith
of the Jew restored itself, and gave him hope for the future,
without which no man can long endure.

Faith and Reason—Feeling and Learning

There were those who were distressed by the emotion-
alizing of Judaism. Rabbinical teachers feared the abuses
to which a too great stress on the role of emotion in religion and the importance of the Zaddik might lead. They
were concerned about the rise of superstitious beliefs, the
use of amulets and the tendency to forget the importance of
Jewish learning that Chassidism seemed to encourage.

In Vilna, seat of learning of Lithuanian Jews, one of
the great intellectual luminaries of the time, Elijah, called
Gaon of Vilna, placed himself and his followers in complete
opposition to Chassidism and threatened its leaders with
excommunication. The Gaon of Vilna saw the need of Jewish life in his time differently, and hoped to minister to it,
not by lessening the importance of Jewish study, but by
making it more inviting to larger numbers. He urged his
students not to engage in hair-splitting disquisitions, but to
discover the true meaning of rabbinical teachings. He
sought to simplify the form of prayers by eliminating many
of the *piyyutim,* sacred poetries that had enlarged and com-
plicated the worship of the Synagogue. He encouraged the

acquisition of secular knowledge as a means of extending the understanding of the world and of deepening the knowledge of Judaism. With these modifications of Jewish attitudes and interests went an uncompromising objection to Chassidism, so that soon there were two camps in Jewish life, the Chassidim and the Misnagdim, those who opposed them. The opposition was at times fierce, although consisting for the most part in the hurling of verbal charges. One of the followers of the Besht, Rabbi Shneor Zalman of Lodi, sought to make peace between the groups by urging the modification of Chassidism to the extent that it be based upon Wisdom (Chochmoh), Understanding (Binoh) and Knowledge (Deah), and was responsible for the founding of the Habad school of Chassidism. In time the bitterness of opposition between the Chassidim and the Misnagdim abated. With the fall of Poland, the areas where Chassidism was strongest were taken over by Austria, as those where the Misnagdim were most numerous, went to Russia.

As a movement Chassidism did much to restore a balance to Jewish life. It created a rich store of folk teachings that brought comfort and guidance to generations of Jews, whose lives had known all too little of light and hope. It challenged the course of rabbinical teachings, and in so doing became a corrective to it. It provided another, and a valid illustration of the capacity of Judaism to speak to the need of the times, and conditions of Jewish living, and thus to preserve both Jew and Judaism.

Reformation—A Little Hope—Disappointment

In Western Europe, for a small moment, light seemed to break through the darkness of Jewish life with the advent of the Protestant Reformation. Martin Luther included among his charges against the Catholic Church that of mistreatment of the Jews. In 1523 Luther wrote a pamphlet entitled *That Jesus Christ Was Born a Jew,* calling attention to the fact that the Jews were the people who had given

the Bible to the world and that Christians ought to act
toward the Jews with love. It was this that made the Jews
of Germany look with sympathy and hope at the rise of
the Reformation in Christendom. But Luther was no different from the papal leader whom he attacked, in one
respect at least, his desire to convert the Jews to Christianity. He had hoped that his approach would result in
mass conversion of the Jews. When this did not happen,
his attitude changed, and he turned in violent attack upon
the Jews, repeating ancient and unfounded accusations
against them, calling upon Christians to burn their homes
and Synagogues, urging the princes to banish them from
their lands. In a sermon just a few days before his death
Luther said: "I say to you lastly, as a countryman, if the
Jews refuse to be converted, we ought not to suffer them or
bear with them any longer." Yet, when Luther translated
the Bible into German he utilized the commentary of the
fourteenth-century scholar, Nicholas de Lyra, who in turn
admitted his debt to the great Jewish commentator, Rashi,
Solomon Yitzchaki of Troyes, whose commentaries had become indispensable to the understanding of Bible and Talmud. In this fashion the learning and Scriptures of the
Jews played a significant role in the Protestant Reformation and helped to transmit a knowledge of the Scriptures
to the Western world.

The Thirty Years' War left central Europe shattered,
both culturally and economically, and divided into numerous duchies and principalities. In some instances, Jews
were granted new privileges so that they might help restore the economy of the ravaged land. Frederick William,
Elector of Prussia, encouraged the Jews, who became the
agents of trade between the various German states. Their
efforts restored commerce and industry in Germany and
helped to lay the foundations of Germany as the great
industrial and cultural center of Europe.

Tolerance—A New Experience

In Holland the Jews were treated with a greater degree of tolerance than anywhere else in Europe. The first communities of Jews in Holland were established by Marranos, who had fled from Spain and Portugal. In Holland they could once again practice their Judaism. German Jews came to Holland in the seventeenth century, and Polish refugees founded a community in 1660. Before the end of the century there were Synagogues, Jewish schools and cemeteries in a number of Dutch cities. The Jews in Holland played an active role in extending Dutch commerce and colonization, and were among those who established the early Dutch settlements in South, Central and North America.

As the Jews in Holland were enabled to practice Judaism and build their Jewish community life, they did not look lightly upon those who wished to use their newfound freedom for untrammeled intellectual expression. Uriel da Costa, reared in Portugal for a career in the Church, became a Jew once again in Amsterdam. His writings, critical of Judaism however, brought upon him the fate of excommunication from the Jewish community. Baruch Spinoza a generation later, free-thinking Jew, incurred the wrath of Jews, who regarded Spinoza's writings as a threat to their newly established community. Excommunicated by the Jewish community, Spinoza earned his livelihood as a lens grinder and wrote philosophical-theological treatises of the greatest importance. In his works he questioned the divine origin of the Jewish laws and Scriptures and placed great stress on the importance of the ethical teachings of Judaism.

Manasseh ben Israel was another of the great figures that arose among Dutch Jewry. As teacher, rabbi and scholar his influence reached beyond Holland, and he helped to re-establish a Jewish community in England. He wrote a book, *The Hope of Israel,* in which he advanced the theory that the Messiah would come after the Jews

were found in every land of the world. He pointed to the
Indians in America as Jews who had made their way from
Asia Minor to the Western Hemisphere; only in England
was there no Jewish settlement. Cromwell was impressed
by this observation and invited Manasseh ben Israel to
England. The discussions aroused by Manasseh's theories
did not at once permit Jews to return to England, but
Marrano Jews who were there were moved to openly declare themselves as Jews. Small groups of Jews began to
settle in England by the end of the seventeenth century.

Walls Do Not Shut Out Forever

A number of factors combined to break down the ghetto
walls, whose restrictions, both physical and intellectual,
had shut off the Jew from the world. These walls were
never altogether tight. The mind and the spirit may pierce
the stone of ignorance and break the chains of bigotry. Jewish scholarship had its influence on Christian thought. In-
trepid Jewish colonizers helped to establish settlements in
the New World. The Bible with its great doctrines of human
freedom, taught men the divine origins of liberty, and fed
the yearning of pilgrim and pioneer, who braved many
dangers that the free life might be established.

This struggle for freedom began among Jews and perhaps for a large part of the world with the work of Moses
Mendelssohn. Young Talmud student of Dessau, Mendelssohn made his way on foot to Berlin in 1742. There he supported himself as a bookkeeper and devoted himself to the
study of languages and philosophy. He saw the necessity
of the Jew knowing the language and literature of the
times and the people among whom he lived. He translated
the first five books of the Bible into German and had them
published with the Hebrew text. He co-operated with his
friends Solomon Dubno and Naphtali Hertz Wessely in
preparing a popular commentary on the Bible. He met a
young German aristocrat, Gotthold Ephraim Lessing, who

published Mendelssohn's *Philosophical Conversations,* which introduced Mendelssohn to the literary world of his time. Mendelssohn influenced Lessing, who became the leading exponent of understanding and good-will toward the Jew. Lessing influenced Mendelssohn, making him feel at home in the world. In Lessing's play *Nathan the Wise,* the example of a noble and high-minded Jew is patterned after Mendelssohn as model. But the way of freedom is never easy. There were Jews in Mendelssohn's day who looked askance at this new liberalism. They wondered if translating the Bible and opening a modern school where young Jews would be taught German was good for the preservation of Judaism. In practice, however, Mendelssohn was completely orthodox. He believed and taught that there should be no change in Jewish observance and ritual. Mendelssohn was not in that sense, then, a founder of the modern movement for reform in Judaism. He did help to pave the way for the liberation of the Jewish spirit. But in Mendelssohn's lifetime political and civil liberation for the Jews was not realized.

The French Revolution and the Napoleonic wars that followed brought the promise of "liberty, equality and fraternity" to the Jews, and in September, 1791, French citizenship was given them. French armies carried the ideal of emancipation for the Jews to other parts of Europe, and new republics were established that carried the promise of equal rights for Jews in their constitutions. In 1806 Napoleon called together a convocation of the leaders of the Jewish communities of France. The convocation was followed by the assembling of a Sanhedrin of Jewish scholars, which Napoleon sought to organize to deal with Jewish questions. The role of Napoleon in these efforts is often characterized as motivated more by a desire for propaganda than the improvement of the position of the Jews.

Passing Promise of Emancipation

For a time, an all too short a time, emancipation came to the Jews, and enlightenment seemed to be the spiritual climate as the nineteenth century began in Europe. Before the middle of the century, however, reaction had canceled out many of the newly acquired rights of the Jew, and anti-Semitism as a political policy was seen to rear its ugly head. For some Jews, the process of emancipation and the securing of their civil rights, tenuous as they were, could only be complete if they discarded their Jewishness altogether. Some of these, eager for acceptance in Christian society, unhappy at meeting new restrictions aimed at the freedom of the Jew, decided that the only way of liberation was through the Church.

Rise of Reform

Other Jews felt that their uncertain liberties were a challenge and presented an opportunity for a fuller and freer Jewish life. Schools were opened, particularly in Germany, where the youth would be given a secular as well as a Jewish education, so that they might be prepared for cultural participation in a free society, and remain knowing, practicing Jews. Men like Israel Jacobson opened one such school in Seesen in 1801, and others were opened in Dessau, Frankfurt am Main, Wolfenbüttel and Cassel. In these schools a type of religious service was organized that sought to make Jewish worship appealing and understandable. The service was shortened, prayers translated into the vernacular were included, musical accompaniment for hymns was added and the sermon became a regular part of the service as a means of instruction in the meaning of Judaism. In other communities, notably Hamburg and Berlin, Temples were established that were not part of a school for young people, where this new type of Jewish worship was offered. Many were attracted to them who had found the services of the Synagogue lacking in meaning and inspiration. The modest reforms in the conduct of worship in these new Temples did much to give renewed vitality to the Synagogue and to restore the capacity of Judaism to meet the changing circumstances of life.

Despite the success of these reforms in stemming the tide of defection from the Synagogue, they met with violent opposition. The orthodox-minded leaders of the Jews inveighed against reforms and reformers, and mistakenly sought the intervention of the government. In 1823, by decree of the Prussian government, the new Temples were closed and reforms in Jewish worship interdicted. The Reform movement did not come to an end. Scholars began to study the basis for the Reform idea in Jewish thought and history. Leopold Zunz, in his classical work, *The Homilies of the Jews, Historically Developed,* sought to prove the rightful place of the sermon in Jewish worship as a means of teaching the understanding of Scriptures, and the inherent ability of Judaism to develop and adapt itself to the needs of life.

Other young men, believing that the restoration of Jewish life and thought would come only from a re-examination of the sources of Jewish knowledge, launched, in 1819, a "Society for the Advancement of the Science of Judaism," and thus began the movement of research and study of Judaism, called *"Wissenschaft des Judentums."* To other lands, in France and England and among the few and sparse settlements of Jews in the United States, the idea of Reform spread. A ferment of interest in Judaism, of questioning the new developments in Jewish life, of studying the backgrounds and origins of the Synagogue and its institutions was brought about by the rise of the Reform movement, which has continued to influence the whole course of Jewish life to the present time.

If governments could interfere with the free practice and development of Judaism, the rights of the Jew were not very secure, and liberalism not very certain in Europe. It was the reaction against liberalism in the middle of the nineteenth century that sent immigrants in large numbers to find new homes and new freedoms in the New World.

Jews in the Western Hemisphere

Jews had lived in Mexico and in Peru under the Portuguese. Many of these Jews had been Marranos, who had hoped to live a free life and practice Judaism in the New World. But the Inquisition of the Portuguese followed them and made their lives difficult, if not impossible. Under the Dutch, conditions were vastly better. As many as six hundred Jews are said to have settled in Recife, Brazil, in 1642, where they helped to establish a Jewish community, built a Synagogue, and fostered trade between Brazil and Holland. Other Jews settled in Surinam, Dutch Guiana, in the Barbados, Curaçao and Jamaica. But war between Holland and Portugal, and the conquest of the colonies by the Portuguese, made it impossible for the Jews to remain in those places.

Jews Come to America

In 1654 the first group of Jews, refugees from the Portuguese attack, sought a haven in the Dutch colony of New Amsterdam in North America. Although not made welcome by the governor of the colony, Peter Stuyvesant, the Dutch West Indies Company ordered that asylum be given to the Jews, and expressed the characteristic Dutch policy of liberalism in insisting that "These people may travel and trade to and in New Netherlands, and live and remain there, providing the poor among them shall be supported by their own nation." In another statement the directors of the Dutch West Indies Company declared: "The consciences of men ought to be free and unshackled, so long as they continue moderate, peaceable, inoffensive and not hostile to government . . . and the consequences have been that the oppressed and persecuted from every country have found among us an asylum from distress. Follow in the same steps and you will be blest." Through the Jews and because of the Jews the struggle for political and spiritual freedom in the New World found expression and champions.

When the British took New Amsterdam from the Dutch and it became New York, there was a tiny Jewish community that had established a cemetery, but had not yet built a Synagogue. In 1682 the Jews worshiped in a rented house, and it was not until 1728 that Congregation Shearith Israel built the first Synagogue to be erected in North America. It stood at what was Broad and Mill streets (South William Street today) in old New York.

Liberty of Conscience

Small Jewish communities were established elsewhere in the colonies, and by the time of the American Revolution there were settlements of Jews in Lancaster and Philadelphia, Pennsylvania; Newport, Rhode Island; Savannah, Georgia; Charleston, South Carolina, as well as in New York. Although their numbers were small, probably no more than three thousand souls, many were ardent supporters of the struggle for liberty, and served as soldiers in the War of the Revolution, or helped to raise the funds needed to carry the Revolution to victory. After the election of George Washington as first President of the United States, the Jewish communities then in existence sent letters of congratulation to Washington and expressed their feelings of loyalty, and willingness to support the newly founded democracy. In his reply to the letter of the Hebrew Congregation of Newport, R. I., Washington wrote: ". . . The citizens of the United States have a right to applaud themselves for having given to mankind examples of an enlarged and liberal policy worthy of imitation. All possess

alike liberty of conscience and immunities of citizenship. . . .”

Pioneers

The number of Jews in the eighteenth-century United
States was less than five thousand among the more than
seven million people that constituted the total population.
As America spread, first beyond the Alleghenies and then
to the Pacific, new towns were founded, and new communities of Jewish settlers were established by the hardy
spirits that made a way through the wilderness. As their
numbers grew the Jews found it necessary to build Synagogues and schools. The peddler settled down and became
shopkeeper at the crossroads that had become a village.
The artisan expanded his back-room shop into the first little
factory. The printer turned his hand press to newspaper
and book publishing. The preacher and teacher were invited from a distant community, sometimes all the way
from their European homes, to take up the work of teaching Judaism in the New World.

Liberalism Finds a Home

For a long time, the Synagogue in America was modeled
after that of Europe; its rabbis and teachers were trained
in European schools and seminaries. The freedom of conscience and of religious practice, the separation of Church
and State, that were the very essentials of American democracy, made it possible for the spirit of reform and liberalism, that had not flourished in Europe, to be revived in
Jewish religious life in America. With the failure of the
Revolution of 1848 in Germany, many liberals, both Jews
and non-Jews, decided that the hope for freedom was lost.
This feeling of despair sent many of them as emigrants to
America, the land where freedom had been established
and liberalism was assured of the right of expression. The

new immigration added greatly to the number and spirit of the Jews in the United States. By 1850 the number of Jews was increased to fifty thousand, and continued to grow as other tides of immigration brought hosts of men and women, driven by poverty and oppression, discrimination and restriction to leave European lands.

Beginnings of Reform Judaism in America

As early as 1824, in Charleston, South Carolina, the attempt was made to inaugurate reforms in the Synagogue service. A group of members of the Beth Elohim Congregation of Charleston asked the vestry of the Congregation to make certain modest reforms in the ritual. The vestry rejected the petition, and twelve of the petitioners decided to form a new congregation, the first Reform congregation in America, known as "The Reformed Society of Israelites." In 1838 the Synagogue of Beth Elohim was destroyed in the Charleston fire, and as a new Synagogue was planned, the idea of uniting the two groups was advanced. The adoption of Reform was urged for the new Synagogue, and encouraged by the preacher and reader of Beth Elohim, the Rev. M. Gustav Posnanski. When the new Synagogue was dedicated, in 1841, it was with victory for the Reform party. The organ had been introduced, the second day observance of holidays abolished, and other reforms were sanctioned in Beth Elohim.

In other communities, influenced by the ideas of Reform, and by the arrival of Jews from Germany who had known something of the Reform movement, "Vereins" or societies were formed, out of which the early Reform Congregations emerged: Har Sinai in Baltimore in 1842, Emanuel of New York in 1845, Keneseth Israel, Philadelphia, in 1856, and Sinai of Chicago in 1860. These groups were made up of laymen, who saw the practical necessity of Reform as a means of giving meaning and vitality to the Synagogue and to Judaism. Rabbinical leaders came from

Europe, where they had seen liberalism fail, and they were
eager to help the new Reform groups grow and find an en-
during place in American life. Max Lilienthal came in 1845,
Isaac Mayer Wise in 1846. David Einhorn became the
leader of the Baltimore Congregation in 1855, and Samuel
Adler was called to New York, Bernard Felsenthal to Chicago in 1858, Samuel Hirsch to Philadelphia in 1866. Although there was opposition from the Orthodox, and at
times the opposition was loud and vigorous, nothing could
stay the progress of Reform, suited as it was to the free
environment of America, and encouraged by its liberal
spirit.

Isaac Mayer Wise was the architect and organizer of
Reform in America. He was convinced that in time the
liberal expression of Judaism would become American Judaism, Judaism for all Jews in America. Toward this end he
sought to unify American Jewish life by organizing, in
1873, the Union of American Hebrew Congregations. This
first union of Congregations sponsored the establishment in
1875 of a rabbinical seminary, the Hebrew Union College,
first school for the training of rabbis to have continuous
existence. As the number of rabbis, trained in America for
American Congregations increased, it was possible for Isaac
Mayer Wise to call together and found the Central Conference of American Rabbis in 1889.

Transfer of Jewish Life

Jewish life in America, fed by the migrations of those
who found living in European lands no longer possible,
continued to flourish and expand. At the close of the nineteenth century and in the early years of the twentieth, the
convulsions of anti-Semitism throughout Europe sent large
masses of Jews to the United States. From Eastern Europe,
principally from Russia, Poland and Rumania some two
million Jews came in the years from 1881 to 1920, and for

eight of those years more than a hundred thousand arrived each year.

These Jews came seeking for the opportunities of freedom; they were eager for education, hard-working and thrifty, determined to forge ahead in the New World. They were pious and orthodox in their religious outlook and practice. They had fled from massacres and restrictions. The Russian May Laws of 1882 had uprooted them, and pogroms from 1881 to 1905 had been responsible for the destruction of many Jewish communities. America became their "promised land" and they came spiritually prepared to realize the best of its promise. This new immigration added more than numbers. In time, as they became rooted in the American scene, they made great contributions to industry and science, art and literature, to the religious and civic life of the United States. New institutions for the perpetuation of Judaism were established. The struggling movement of Conservative Judaism, seeking only a limited modification of traditional Judaism, was strengthened and stimulated. Orthodox schools and seminaries were established, and as the need arose, philanthropic institutions were established in which all Jewish groups participated.

Zionism

As Jewish life in America was marked by growth and creativity, Jewish life in Europe showed signs of decline and dissolution. The outbreak of anti-Semitism in France at the time of the Dreyfus trial, convinced a brilliant young journalist, Theodor Herzl, of the untenability of Jewish life in Europe. Herzl felt that if a Dreyfus could be falsely accused merely because he was a Jew, and in a nation that he regarded as the most civilized in Europe, there was no hope for Jews elsewhere in Europe. Herzl reacted by writing the *Judenstaat (A Jewish State)*, urging the establishment of a modern Jewish state. He followed this with the organization of the Zionist Congress in 1897, and became the leader of the Zionist movement, whose goal was "to secure for the Jewish people a publicly recognized, legally secured home in Palestine." The movement had not originated with Herzl; unknown to him Moses Hess had written *Rome and Jerusalem,* and Hirsch Kalischer had published *Derishat Zion (The Quest for Zion),* in 1862, urging the re-establishment of a national home in Palestine. Perez Smolenskin and Leo Pinsker had urged national revival for the Jews a quarter of a century before, and even thoughtful Christians like Laurence Oliphant and George Eliot had written of the revival of a Jewish settlement in Palestine. In 1884 the Hoveve Zion had been established to further the Jewish colonization of Palestine. Baron Edmond de Rothschild gave financial support to the establishment of Jewish colonies in Palestine, and recruited by the BILU, Russian Jewish student movement, Jews were settled in 1882 in four Rothschild-aided colonies.

While Zionism was hailed with enthusiasm by Russian Jewry, it met with great opposition or indifference elsewhere. German Jewry, for the most part feeling secure, and unwilling to accept the manifestations of anti-Semitism as more than a passing phase of political life, was loath to encourage the Zionist movement. Yet the time was to come when anti-Semitism as a weapon of Hitler and his National Socialism was to destroy the Jew, not only in Germany, but in a large part of Europe, and make Palestine one of the few havens in the world to which the German Jews and others, the victims of his cruelties, might escape. In America, where Jews had every reason to feel secure, and were rapidly taking root in the new, free world, the idea of a re-established Jewish state in Palestine made little appeal. Many Reform rabbis opposed the idea of nationalism as contrary to the universalistic teachings of Judaism. They regarded the existence of Jews in many lands as fortuitous; as the means by which Judaism could be a world influence in the spread of the teachings of brotherhood and moral living, as the universal necessities for the creation of world peace.

Jewish Homeland—From Dream to Uncertain Reality

The Balfour Declaration was secured from the British government before the end of the First World War through the efforts of such leaders as Rabbi Stephen S. Wise and Justice Louis D. Brandeis in America, and Dr. Chaim Weizmann in England. It read: "His Majesty's Government view with favour the establishment in Palestine of a national home for the Jewish people and will use their best endeavours to facilitate the achievement of this object, it being clearly understood that nothing shall be done which may prejudice the civil and religious rights of existing non-Jewish communities in Palestine or the rights and status enjoyed by Jews in any other country."

At the Versailles Peace Conference that followed the end of World War I, Jews from the United States, England, France and some East European countries were represented by a Comité des Délégations Juives headed by Louis Marshall of America. Largely as a result of the urging of the East European representatives, a plan for the protection of minority rights was advanced. The plan was adopted for all minority groups, Jewish and non-Jewish. Out of the Versailles Conference also came the idea of mandated territories, with England given the mandate for Palestine. In 1920 Sir Herbert Samuel was appointed the first High Commissioner for Palestine. But Britain's position was always an ambivalent one; it had made promises to the Arabs to win their support, and these promises were often contrary to the intention of the Balfour Declaration. Despite the fact that Emir Feisal, Arab prince, had publicly declared that Palestine was to be a Jewish homeland, many Arab leaders opposed its creation.

Zion Is Rebuilt

In the face of uncertainties and difficulties, large-scale operations were undertaken by the Jews in the effort to rebuild and resettle the ancient and long-neglected land of Palestine. Many Jews left European communities to help in translating the ideal of Zion rebuilt into reality. Unused as many were to the back-breaking labor, they nevertheless set themselves to the task of reclaiming the fields that had become a desert. They drained swamps, built new colonies and introduced modern methods of agriculture. They set up a system of health and education, established a Hebrew University, made Hebrew the language of the people, built new cities and brought the ideas of progress and democracy to what had been an almost forgotten land among the backward peoples of the Middle East. At times riots broke out against the new settlers. Investigating commissions were sent to discover the cause of the troubles. The investigations did not improve the position of the Jews; land purchase was made more difficult and immigration was limited. Sadly enough, all this happened when the threats to Jewish life in Europe were becoming more real and the need for a haven more pressing.

Decline of European Jewry

Between World War I and World War II the position of the Jews in Europe worsened. The Russian Revolution and the rise of the Soviets did not bring liberation to the Jews of Russia. While the Communists declared that anti-Semitism would not be tolerated, the religious life of the Jews and with it their cultural institutions were severely restricted. Only antireligious Jewish activity was encouraged. In the new Poland, Jews became the victims of the failing economy of the nation, that did not use its new-found opportunities of freedom to become a democracy or to encourage democratic practices. Jewish survival in Poland depended in large measure on relief from American Jews. In Germany, Jews were made the scapegoats on whom it was convenient to blame the failure of the postwar economy. Hitler made the Jews the target of his propaganda, and when he and his Nazi government assumed power in 1933, they set about to achieve the destruction of the Jews of Germany and Jews everywhere, as he planned his campaign to conquer the world. This should have been a warning to the nations that minimized the Hitler threat by regarding what he was doing to the Jews as an internal problem of Germany alone.

Warning Unheeded—The Dreadful Price the World Paid

As many Jews were to be doomed by Hitler, so a large part of the world was to be ravaged by his plans to spread the Nazi rule. In no small measure, World War II was the consequence of the failure to curb Hitler and to stop his march to power before he succeeded in destroying much of Europe and involving most of the nations of the world in conflict. The failure of the conscience of men to speak out was signalized in November, 1938, when Hitler organized the burning of every Synagogue in Germany and drove the Jews of every community into concentration camps, their only crime being their Jewishness. When World War II ended and the price of the devastation wrought by the Nazis was added up, not the least part of the price was the destruction of six million Jews, one-third of the total Jewish population of the world.

No Other Home

From the ruins of Europe and the destruction of Jewish life some escaped. With faith in the future they turned toward Palestine, and in the face of almost every conceivable obstacle—lack of means of transportation, a Bri-

tish administration that had practically closed the doors to
Jewish immigration into Palestine, Arab antagonism—they
were determined to share in the building of a homeland
for Jews who had no other home to which they might
return. The Haganah, Jewish self-defense organization that
had come into being in the time of the Arab riots, engaged
in the work of smuggling the escapees into Palestine. During World War II, the Palestinian Jewish soldiers had
played a heroic part in aiding the British in withstanding
the Nazi invasion of North Africa. From their limited numbers, 25,000 Jewish volunteers served with the British
forces. In Arab lands at the same time there was open
co-operation with Nazi and Fascist forces. With the war
over, the Palestinian Jews found themselves in conflict with
British policy and administration. Despite the conflict no
Jew failed to find help, home and encouragement once he
was in sight of Palestine's shore, and the hands of the Jewish settlers could reach out to him in welcome and rescue.
The British sought to deport these desperate remnants of
Nazi destruction. The administration of Palestine became
more and more confused. Open conflict with the Jewish
settlements in Palestine and its leadership broke out. Par-
tition plans were conceived, new restrictions against Jewish
settlement and development of Palestine were promulgated.

Israel—The Jewish State

In 1947 the United Nations divided Palestine into a
Jewish State, an Arab State, and an International Zone
which included Jerusalem. Despite Arab opposition to this
plan, on May 14, 1948 a Jewish State bearing the name of
Israel was proclaimed. The Arab countries proceeded to
attack the new Jewish State, which protected itself suc-
cessfully against the assault. The war with the Arab League
countries was ended in January, 1949 by United Nations
mediation.

American Jewry to the Rescue

During this troubled period that followed World War II, the American Jewish community was not unmindful of its obligations. In the greatest demonstration of private philanthropy on record, American Jews gave many millions of dollars for the support of the work of the American Jewish Joint Distribution Committee and the United Palestine Appeal. The work included the relief and rehabilitation of the Jews of Europe, aid in rebuilding Palestine and the settlement there of the largest number of escapees from European lands, the resettlement of refugees and displaced persons in America, South American countries and other lands that would grant them the right of entry. The government of the United States took a very active role in seeking to influence Great Britain in reopening Palestine to Jewish immigration. When the establishment of the Jewish State was declared, the United States, under the leadership of President Truman, was the first to accord recognition, and has since given substantial aid and encouragement to Israel, re-established commonwealth of the Jews and outpost of democracy in the Middle East.

Mid-Twentieth-Century Picture of Jewish Life

The mid-twentieth century found the Jews of the world greatly diminished in numbers and located for the most part in two important Jewish communities, those of the United States and Israel. Except for relatively small Jewish communities in England, France and Italy, Jewish life is practically nonexistent in Europe. The Jews in Russia and the satellite countries of Russia lead a very uncertain existence, know little of Judaism, and play no role in developing a positive kind of Jewish life. The Jewish communities in North Africa and in Arab lands are in the process of disintegration, with migration to Israel as their only hope. Small communities of Jews in South America, South Africa and Australia lead a peaceful, but not very significant existence. In the United States, it is estimated, there are five and a half million Jews. Theirs is a very virile, active and well-organized kind of Jewish life. In their religious life they are found in three great groups, the Orthodox, Conservative and Reform Synagogues. They have numerous institutions for the training of rabbis and teachers for their Synagogues and the religious schools that are part of the Synagogues. Many communal institutions of welfare, education, and cultural and social activity receive the support of all branches of the Jewish community. Changing conditions and practical necessity have called forth widespread sympathy and support for the work of rebuilding Israel as a Jewish State, and all groups in American Jewry have come to regard aid to Zion as compatible with their Americanism and their Judaism.

Resurgence of the Synagogue as Center of Jewish Life

In the mid-century period there was and continues to be a marked resurgence of interest in the Synagogue as the central institution of Jewish life in America. The number of Synagogues is on the increase, many new Synagogues have been established, especially in the new suburban communities, and Synagogue membership has shown tremendous gains in the period from 1946 to 1956. Accompanying the heightened interest in the Synagogue goes an increasing interest in Jewish education. More children, young people and adults are enrolled in classes and groups for Jewish education than at any previous time in American Jewish history.

Jewish life in America in the second half of the twentieth century is a demonstration of the proposition that Judaism and freedom are indivisible. As freedom may well be regarded as the first commandment of Judaism ("I am the Lord thy God who brought thee out of the land of Egypt, out of the house of bondage"), it must be regarded as the indispensable factor making for Jewish survival and development. As Judaism sought to free the mind and spirit of man from the shackles of superstition, so the Jew, bearer of the message of man as the child of God, endowed with freedom, and with faith in the future, has flourished in the free environment, spreading the influence of his message and encouraging the progress of mankind.

II — Basic Concepts of Judaism

Even the barest outline of Jewish history must show the relatedness of Jew and Judaism. Judaism is the historical result of the spiritual experience of the Jewish people. Without the sense of destiny involved in the Jewish search for the knowledge of God (*daas Elohim*—the knowledge of God—one of the Hebrew terms for religion) the survival of the Jew and the development of Judaism cannot be explained. A definition of Judaism must always fall short of the goal. We cannot fully understand the meaning of Judaism without knowing the historical role of the Jew as the instrument of its creation. We cannot fully appreciate the meaning of Judaism without realizing its universal import. While Judaism, because of its developing, dynamic nature resisted fixed characterization in dogmatic statement, it was never lacking in basic beliefs that gave structure to its spiritual constitution. Upon this structure were built the life and thought of the people, from it came the influences that were to spread a sense of living faith in God and His moral purposes, to a large portion of the world's population. The understanding of these basic concepts and their application is no less important in the modern world than they were in the ancient world in which they had their origin. Time has tested the validity of Jewish concepts, experience has deepened their meaning and the ever-present need of man for spiritual security in an uncertain world has been the warrant for their preservation.

The Idea of God

The Jewish idea of God is based upon the concept of the absolute unity of God. As the Jew proclaims, "Hear O Israel, the Lord our God, the Lord is One," he does more than assert the unity of God; he declares the unity of the world of man, of the law of right and justice, which is one for all men. In His unity, Judaism seeks to describe God as creator, source of life; as unfailing law, regulating the origin and organization of matter; as the perfection of all qualities of spirit and form. God is thus as close to man as feeling, as near as the outreach of his spirit for the source of its being, as concerned for the welfare of man as is the father for the child.

Judaism teaches the moral nature of God, that the holiness of God finds expression in righteousness and justice, in love and in truth. Man comes to recognize God through the intuitive powers of conscience, and serves God through his desire to do righteously, to love mercy and to bear himself as a child of God. Thus Judaism advances the idea of the universal God, God of all mankind and for all men. The ethical involvement of man in recognizing the moral nature of God provides the basic definition of Judaism as ethical monotheism and sanction for social justice. Belief in God calls for more than faith in His reality; it demands moral commitment that is expressed in the affirmations of moral living for men and nations. In this connection Solomon Freehof points out in his introduction to *Reform Jewish Practice:* "The foundation of Jewish religious life is Jewish practice upon which are built habits of mind and attitudes to the universe. It is a case of: 'we will do and then we will hear.' First we obey God's commandments and then we learn to understand God's nature. We do not begin with theology, we *arrive* at theology. This is the basic Jewish way."

As our knowledge of man, the world and the universe grows, our understanding of God increases. Judaism, as science does, teaches the orderliness of life, the laws by which substance and energy, light and power operate with unfailing regularity. This is not conceivable as a system without a Systematizer, as a conglomeration of accidental events without central idea or plan. Judaism, in teaching God as Ribbono shel Olam, "Master of the universe," seeks to establish God as the source and responsible power who daily renews the works of creation. As man turns to God he finds in Him the explanation for the universe and for his own character, and the integrity of his personality as a child of God.

Concept of Man

As Judaism teaches the universal God, single cause and law of the universe, so it designates man as child of God, member of a single mankind. Even as nature is varied in all of its magnificent differences of colors, forms and capacities, yet is one in its essential creativity, so Judaism teaches that man is one, despite his varied origins and characteristics. The Bible, speaking of man, Adam, as gathered from the dust of the earth, of all kinds and from all the parts of the world, seeks to make us understand the essential unity of mankind.

The unity of mankind as taught by Judaism consists of more than common origin. Man's nature and destiny mark him as a being seeking to realize the nobler capacities of his personality. In describing man as created in the image of God, Judaism suggests man's endowment with that spiritual quality that makes him God-aspiring, seeking the perfection of life and character. In this spiritual quality is found the soul of man, sensitive part of his being, reaching for the stars while his feet may tread the dust of his origins. There is an optimism and an infinite preciousness to be found in this being possessed of personality and seeking to express it by ennobling it. The rabbis teach that man may well say, "The whole world was created for my sake . . ." and in consequence "He who saves a single human life is accounted as one who saves a whole world, and he who destroys a single life is as one who destroys a whole world." In this consideration for the worth and integrity of every man's personality is found the Jewish love of life, the desire to make the most of it; hope for the future and belief in the perfectibility of man and his world. Man must therefore possess the powers of the free soul and the free mind, that he may be a free person. Moral choice and moral behavior are possible only for the free person, as is enunciated in the first of the Ten Commandments, "I am the Lord, thy God, who brought thee out of the land of Egypt, out of the house of bondage." (Exodus 20:2)

Because man is free, he is free to choose between the good and the evil. "See I have set before thee this day life and good and death and evil . . . the blessing and the curse; therefore choose life, that thou mayest live." (Dt. 30:19) Man's relation to God has endowed him with moral capacity, with judgment, with knowledge and incentive to make the right choice, the choice which will bless his life with the greater gifts of goodness. The free man may also fail to make the right choice, but he is not condemned to suffer without hope for redemption from the consequences of error. Man may retrace his steps and start over again, achieving in his second attempt the goal he missed in the first. In repentance for error, in the recognition of sin and its rejection as the wrong course of life, man returns to God and goodness. This is the power of *teshuvoh*, or repentance, or return, through which man may cure his fault, redeem himself from the corruption into which he may have fallen. In this power of self-redemption from the sin of wrongdoing is contained the key to the progress of man as individual and as society. Man's search for the truth helps

him to better recognize the life-preserving and life-
ennobling qualities that influence human conduct. Man's
struggle toward a happier social order is motivated by the
feeling that it is in his power to be partner with God in the
creation of a better world.

Place and Purpose of Israel

In referring to Israel we use the term to describe the
whole Jewish people, not any portion of it, such as that
contained in the modern State of Israel. It is this people
that has made a career of being the bearer of the knowledge
of God and His ways to the world. It is this people that
felt itself called to serve God. The Prophet Isaiah describes
the call and its duties:

Behold, My servant, whom I uphold;
Mine elect, in whom My soul delighteth;
I have put My spirit upon him
He shall make the right to go forth to the nations. . . .
I the Lord have called thee in righteousness
And have taken hold of thy hand,
And kept thee and set thee for a covenant of the people
For a light to the nations. (Is. 42:1,6)

To discharge this special vocation, Israel had to feel a
sense of high moral purpose in the world. In this feeling of
high moral purpose, in this concept of the chosenness of
Israel, there is no notion of racial superiority, no suggestion
that in the sight of God there are some peoples more entitled to his love than others. The mother's vocation is a
chosen one, chosen by God for womankind, chosen by the
woman herself in fulfilling her nature, yet her chosenness
does not make her children, be they men or women, in-
ferior before God or less entitled to His love. Israel, like
womankind, has often chosen to suffer in order to discharge

the vocation for which it was called. The world at times
turned a deaf ear to Israel's teaching, and in refusing the
teaching rejected the teacher. But the example of a people
dedicated to convey to the world a knowledge of God, at
other times influenced men in spite of themselves. The
moral values taught by Judaism became the moral foundations of a large portion of the civilized world. The Scriptures of the Jew became the Bible, revered and referred
to as the Holy Book by many non-Jews. Certainly this spiritual career had its effect upon the Jewish people, making
them feel that in the call to service they were called to
live worthily, to conduct themselves always with the consciousness that the eyes of the world were upon them. The
Talmud describes the characteristics of the Jewish people
as "chastity and purity of life, benevolence and active love
for humanity." While Jews and Judaism have not sought to
win men from following other religious teachings, they have
not denied them entrance into the household of Israel. Often
the example of a people that has persisted in its advocacy
of the ideals of one God, one mankind and one moral law
for all the world has won men to appreciate the spiritual
power of this people, and made them want to be joined
with them.

Israel's purpose in the world was not to win all men
to Israel or even to Israel's faith, but to God. In the prayer
book we have this stated for us in a prayer for the closing
service of the Day of Atonement:

> Endow us, our Guardian, with strength and patience
> for our holy mission. Grant that all the children of Thy
> people may recognize the goal of our changeful career,
> so that they may exemplify by their zeal and love of
> mankind the truth of Israel's watchword: One humanity
> on earth, even as there is but one God in heaven. En-
> lighten all that call themselves by Thy name with the
> knowledge that the Sanctuary of wood and stone, which

first crowned Zion's hill, was but a gate through which
Israel would step out into the world, to reconcile all
mankind unto Thee! (U.P., II, pp. 332-365)

Torah—Moral Law and Learning

Judaism, although defined as the religion of the people
of Israel, has its wider universal aspects. So Torah, which
began as the revelation of God unto Israel, as the covenant
between Israel and God, came to have universal import
as the moral law by which all men might live, a moral
code by which all nations might be governed. This is the
unique contribution of Judaism as the religion of the Jewish people, that the revelation of God's ways was given, not
to one man, but to the whole people, and not to them alone,
but through them to the whole of mankind. Torah, or religious teaching, is the means of conveying what might be
called the law of God to the understanding of man. Thus
it is that Torah has come to be more than a book or a collection of books, more than a scroll of the law and more
than law itself. It is man's total record of his search for the
knowledge of God and to it must be added the teaching
of every age as it seeks the clearer light of the understanding of God's way. Through all the ages of Jewish life, Torah
was the means of instruction, and provided the education
that was to bring the children of men closer to God. Faith
was not to be the product of blind acceptance; it was to be
the goal of the searching, knowing and ever increasing understanding of the spirit. For centuries there was no distinction in Jewish life between education and religious education, for all knowledge led to the understanding of God's
ways. In the Synagogue, instruction and prayer were joined
in worship and formed the twin lanes of approach to God.
The Synagogue thus became a house of study as well as a
house of prayer. The study of the Torah became the duty
of every person, and it was the obligation of the community
to provide the means of study, the place and the teachers.

It was this emphasis on study and the need to acquire the knowledge of God that influenced the cultural and social patterns of the world. One of the great contributions of Judaism to the world has been the idea of the importance of education and the obligation of the community to provide educational opportunities to all its members. This came to be a characteristic of the democratic community, and general education to be regarded as the right of free people everywhere.

Salvation and Social Responsibility

In the early history of the Jewish people, the concept of salvation was expressed in terms of the people's prayer that God might save them from their enemies. Later, salvation is expressed as the hope for survival and restoration of the people. The Prophet Zachariah spoke of God's promise of redemption and the return of the people from exile to their own land. "Behold I will save my people from the east country, and from the west country; and I will bring them and they shall dwell in the midst of Jerusalem; and they shall be My people, and I will be their God in truth and righteousness." (Zech. 8:7) The restoration of the people was coupled with the resurrection of the dead, as in Ezekiel 37: "I will open your graves and cause you to come out of your graves, and I will bring you into the Land of Israel." And in Daniel (12:2) the idea of immortality is suggested in this connection: "And many of them that sleep in the dust shall awake, some to everlasting life." These references to the salvation of the people and the salvation of the individual in a life after death did not assume the form or importance of a central doctrine in Jewish teaching. The clear direction of Jewish thought was that salvation was to be regarded as a human enterprise, that whatever survival was to be sought in the world was to be in terms of humanity. The emphasis is upon the social aspects of salvation rather than upon the individual, as Kaufmann Kohler

indicates in his *Jewish Theology*. "The truth of the matter
is that the aim and end of Judaism is not so much the salvation of the soul in the hereafter as the salvation of humanity in history." Salvation became something more than
a hoped-for state in the hereafter; it must be a worked-for
condition of human society. Leo Baeck in his *Essence of
Judaism* defines salvation in Judaism as "a duty imposed
by God, which man has to fulfill."

The fulfillment of social responsibility is Judaism's road
to salvation. This is a road wide enough for every man, and
one that can link all peoples in a common purpose. Social
responsibility reaches all the way from the need for fair
dealing between man and man, calling for just weights and
balances, protection of the weak, fair treatment of the
worker, to the organization of society so that poverty and
oppression and war may be eliminated from the experience
of the human race. The road of social responsibility is one
that leads from God to man and from man to God. In the
Holiness Code of Leviticus 19 we are commanded: "Ye
shall be holy, for I the Lord your God am holy," and this
link of holiness between man and God has added to it the
many links of duty that bind man to man, and move him
toward fulfillment of the command, "Thou shalt love thy
neighbor as thyself." In Judaism we have this combination
of the commandment to love one's neighbor and the duty
to establish justice in dealing with him. This is the kind of
social responsibility, demanding of all men as the children
of God the understanding and appreciation of that law of
mutuality, which asks as much for one's neighbor as for
one's self. For the fulfillment of this kind of social responsibility we have the help of our God-given powers to perfect
all things as His partners in the process of creating a nobler
world and a happier society. We are not dependent upon
miraculous intervention, nor are we justified in postponing
our hopes for human salvation to the hereafter. Every day
is our opportunity for salvation, every action can contribute

to bringing near or delaying the establishment of the kingdom of God on earth.

Prayer and Worship

"The Lord is nigh unto all who call upon Him, to all that call upon Him in truth." (Ps. 145:18) Thus Judaism teaches in the words of the Psalmist the nearness of God to man, man's power to reach God, the use of the instrumentality of prayer to express man's aspiration. The Hebrew word for prayer, Tefiloh, suggests the sense of yearning and appeal that turns man toward God. Thus, when man prays, he expresses in positive fashion his faith, faith in God and faith in himself. "Cast thy burden upon the Lord and He will sustain thee." (Ps. 55:23) suggests neither the total weakness of the helpless, who have no power to rise above weakness, nor the arrogance of those who feel that everything lies within the power of their own arms. The ethical optimism of Judaism is expressed in prayer that teaches that there is hope for man and that the nearness of God, the consciousness of His presence gives to man the power to overcome evil, to surmount sorrow, to turn away from frustration, to achieve that victory of the spirit which refuses to be daunted by the transient defeats of time and circumstance.

The Book of Psalms in the Bible, expressing all the varied conditions that prompt men to pray, has become the prayer book and the hymn book of men and women scattered over large areas of the world. From it men have learned to pray, not only when in need of help, which for many would seem the only time to pray, but in times of great joy, in the mood of thanksgiving, in the outpouring of the happy soul. In simple, prayer as Judaism teaches it is the language of the soul to be used in conversation with God in every circumstance of living; as a cry for help, "Save me O God; for the waters are come in even unto the soul"

(Ps. 69:2); as the praise of the thankful spirit, "It is a good thing to give thanks unto the Lord . . . for Thou, Lord, hast made me glad through Thy work" (Ps. 92:2,5); as the recognition of the greatness and goodness of God, "The Lord is good to all; and His tender mercies are over all His works" (Ps. 145:9); as the contemplative expression of wonder, of trust, of the love of God, "The heavens declare the glory of God . . ." (Ps. 19:2), "The Lord is my shepherd; I shall not want" (Ps. 23:1), "How precious is Thy loving kindness, O God! And the children of men take refuge in the shadow of Thy wings." (Ps. 36:8)

As Judaism taught the indispensable value of the power of prayer as a means of lifting man toward God, so it made the collective use of prayer in worship a means of making the community conscious of the presence and place of God in their lives. The transition from the sacrificial altar to the Synagogue as house of prayer was accomplished even before the Synagogue was established, as the prophet urged, "Seek ye the Lord while He is near." (Is. 55:6) Even when the Temple was restored and the sacrificial cult re-established, the local Synagogue continued its important function as a place of regular worship; the kind of worship described in the Talmud as *avodah sheh bah-lev*—"the service of the heart." This represented the great contribution of Judaism to the progress of religious practice. Public worship became the means of religious expression in which all might participate, it provided a time and place for prayer in which all, wise and simple, young or old, in need of help or able to help others, could share in the service of God. This universal appeal and opportunity of worship came to influence the expression of almost every form of religion and made men aware of religious values as the basis of community living.

The Problem of Good and Evil

Every person who contemplates the meaning of religion comes at one time or another to confront the problem of good and evil in the world and in human experience. Some avoid the problem by denying the existence of evil, by declaring that it is an illusion. Judaism has never done so. It points clearly and unequivocally to the presence of evil, the possibility of evil, the threat of evil, the practice of evil. "See, I have set before thee this day life and good and death and evil." (Dt. 30:15) All the moral injunctions of Judaism, the "Thou shalts" urging the way of goodness, the "Thou shalt nots" urging the avoidance of the evil way, are the recognition that there is evil in the world. The soundness of this approach to life is borne out when we examine the nature of living organisms. To declare that there can be no pollution of the public water supply because there is no evil, no disease-bearing bacillae, is to be blind to the point of self-destruction. Judaism says there is evil, there is the danger of evil-doing, there is the threat to life that disease may bear, therefore be warned, take measures to meet the evil, seek the prevention and the cure of disease. "To depart from evil is understanding." (Job 28:28) This is the great contribution of Jewish thought to the moral advancement of mankind; that it teaches that man can avoid and eradicate the evil. Constantly repeated is the Biblical injunction, "So shalt thou put away (eradicate) the evil from the midst of thee." (Dt. 13:6) Man has a choice to make and the power to improve the conditions of living by making the right choice.

The optimism involved in the idea of the moral choice does not free us altogether from the besetting concern with the problem of the innocent who suffer, of the righteous who are molested, of the wicked who seem to prosper, of a world created by a God of goodness, yet marred by so much that is ugly and painful. The Book of Job is the great Jewish classic that dramatizes the problem of "Why do the righteous suffer?" and it provides one answer at least, that it is not due to some hidden sin, as the friends of Job seek to suggest. The second answer is found in the great affirmation of faith, "But as for me, I know that my Redeemer liveth." (Job 19:25) This is the promise that man can and will find redemption from present suffering, that through struggle and sacrifice man rises from the slough of despair to mount the way of hope for a better day. It is the recognition of God, the acceptance of His presence in the operation of the universe that makes this faith in the ultimate good give us the power to rise above the present and seemingly inexplicable suffering and sorrow.

> Lo, these are but the outskirts of His ways;
> And how small a whisper is heard of Him!
> But the thunder of His mighty deeds who can
> understand? (Job 26:14)

> And unto man He said:
> Behold the fear of the Lord, that is wisdom
> And to depart from evil is understanding (Job 28:28)

Summarizing this attitude of Jewish faith in God, in man and in the future of human society, Abba Hillel Silver in *Where Judaism Differed* (page 259) makes it abundantly clear that it is man's duty, as Judaism teaches it, neither to refuse to see evil when it occurs, nor to resign himself to the acceptance of it, but to eradicate it, and with it the suffering and pain that afflict mankind. If he does not succeed in doing so today, he must not desist from trying until he achieves in whole or in part the goal of his moral efforts.

It is not enough to improve oneself; one must seek to improve one's environment. The only refuge from the cruel wrongs of the world is the effort to set them aright. There is no ethics of resignation in Judaism. There are certain evils which man *cannot* eradicate. He cannot do away with death or the accidental tragedies of life. They are inherent in the very structure of human existence. But man can reduce the incidence of disease and accidents. He can lessen pain and physical suffering. Man can also put an end to moral evils. He can eradicate poverty and war—among the chief sources of human misery and suffering. He can eliminate the evils of illiteracy, of bigotry, of exploitation, of inequality.

Life and Death

"Therefore choose life" (Dt. 30:19) expresses the Jewish attitude toward life. It is the gift of God and all the commandments with which a man is charged have the single purpose of helping man to live a good life; "which if a man do, he shall live by them." (Lev. 18:5) The Bible is concerned with life upon earth and has little and rare reference to life after death. The prophets constantly urge men so to live as to create a good human society, based upon justice and righteousness. When they hold before man a picture of that life in the time to come, the Messianic era is not of the world of the hereafter, but of this world, where

With righteousness shall he judge the poor
And decide with equity for the meek of the land
   (Is. 11:4)

For the earth shall be full of the knowledge of the Lord,
As the waters cover the sea. (Is. 11:9)

Man is to find peace not in death or in the life after death —"the work of righteousness shall be peace and the effect of righteousness, quietness and confidence forever." (Is. 32:17) And nations shall learn to live in peace as they follow the ways of God—"they shall beat their swords into plowshares and their spears into pruning hooks." (Is. 2:4)

When the Bible does make reference to a future life it suggests a resurrection of the people of Israel, as the Prophet Ezekiel, prophet of the period of exile portrays a revived and restored people, returning from exile, and re-established in their own native land: "Behold, I will open your graves and cause you to come up out of your graves, O My people, and I will bring you into the land of Israel. ... (Ezek. 37:12) And I will put My spirit in you, and ye shall live, and I will place you in your own land. . . ." (Ezek. 37:14) Beyond this conception of the restored people, there is but the suggestion of the immortality of the soul of man:

> In the way of righteousness is life,
> And in the pathway thereof there is no death.
>   (Prov. 12:28)

Rabbi Abba Hillel Silver in his *Where Judaism Differed* (page 266) points out in this connection: "It is remarkable to note the extraordinary reticence of the Bible and the Mishnah on the subjects of death, resurrection, immortality, the hereafter, the Judgement Day in the after life, Heaven and Hell and the Messiah—subjects which occupied so large a place in the religions of the Near East, the Greco-Roman world, and Christianity."

In Judaism death is neither feared nor praised. There is no cult of the dead, no worship of the dead, no prayers for the dead, no saints to be revered and besought in death. Death is regarded as incidental to life, part of the process of birth, growth and decay. "The dust returneth to the earth as it was, And the spirit returneth unto God who gave it" (Eccl. 12:7) suggests in ancient thought what we think of in modern terms "as the indestructibility of matter," and to which we might add, surely "the imperishability of the spirit."

It is this love of life and the refusal to be frightened by death that characterizes Judaism as the religion of life, as a way of life that would have man make the most of living.

Even when the Jew is sorrowed by death, he rises in the Congregation, not to pray for the dead, for such is not the purpose of the Kaddish prayer recited by the mourner, but to sanctify the name of God. He expresses his undaunted faith in life, and his unwavering confidence that God is the God of life, as he says: "And may He speedily establish His Kingdom of righteousness on earth."

III — Institutions and Practices of Judaism

The Synagogue

The Synagogue is the oldest institution of Judaism and Jewish life. It came into being out of the felt need of the Jewish people in the period of the first exile in Babylonia, possibly during the third or fourth century B.C.E., and has remained the central institution of Jewish life. Its remarkable and vital characteristics may be sensed in the various terms used in reference to it. One of the oldest: Bes Am— "House of the People"—suggests the social and democratic character of the Synagogue, a place for all the people; a place where all the people might participate in the expression of their Judaism, in learning its meaning, in aspiring to its understanding, in seeking the knowledge of the ways in which they might make it an influence in their lives and in the life of the community.

The destruction of the Temple in Jerusalem was responsible for the dissolution of the ancient sacrificial cult. While there was no altar and no organized priesthood there could be no sacrifices. The rise of the Synagogue marked the end of one form of religious practice and the beginning of another, more advanced form; for the Synagogue served the inner and spiritual needs of the people as well as their social needs, their desire to retain a sense of group integrity. The Synagogue in time was found everywhere, in Palestine, even in Jerusalem during the period of the second Temple and wherever there was a community of Jews. Jews came to the Synagogue to pray, and this every Jew could do, for it was a Bes-ha-Tefiloh, a "House of Prayer," where all were alike in their need to seek God in prayer, and all alike had equal opportunity to do so. Prayer in the Synagogue did not require the presence of an official leader of prayer, as the sacrificial cult required the presence of the priest in the Temple. All engaged in prayer, silent or with voices raised in accents of praise. Sincerity in prayer was the only special qualification for its practice.

Synagogue as Place of Learning

Because the Scriptures, the recorded word of God as it was transmitted by His inspired hearers, played so important a role in the guidance of the Jew, the Synagogue was the place where he came to hear the holy words of God repeated and expounded. Thus the Synagogue became the Bes-ha-Midrash, the "House of Study," the place where men would gather to acquire understanding of the ways in which they were to walk and work as children of God. Young and old were required to learn about Judaism, to study its moral requirements so that understanding would prompt them to fulfillment. The Synagogue as house of study became the first public school in the sense that education was a requirement of all, an obligation of the community to provide, so that all might have knowledge of the ways of God and walk in them. There was always a school in the Synagogue. (The Synagogue is still referred to as "Schul" from the German for school.) Worship included instruction. The sermon began as the means by which the learned taught the meaning of Scriptures and its application to life. If there was an aristocracy in the Synagogue it was the aristocracy of learning, and leadership was accorded to the learned. The title of Rabbi was conferred by the people, who, in recognition of their learned teachers, addressed them as Rabee—"My master—my teacher." Even much of the architecture of the Synagogue derives from its use as a place of learning. The Ark, Tebah, or Aron Hakodesh, was the receptacle in which the Scrolls of the Law were kept. The raised platform, or Bimah, was the place from which the scrolls were read, and the pulpit from which their meaning was interpreted. The tablets of the commandments above the ark suggested the ethical importance of the teachings of Judaism. The perpetual light that burned in the Synagogue was the symbol of the light and understanding that Judaism sought to spread in the lives of those who came under its influence. It was an ever-burning light, since the light of knowledge and understanding was a constant need of man.

Synagogue as Center for Social Welfare

Learning, however it was glorified in Judaism, without practice would have been an empty thing. The Synagogue as Bes-ha-Keneses brought the people together to help one another, to benefit from the practice of their Judaism. As Bes-ha-Keneses the Synagogue was the first social center, and the first center for organized philanthropy. The poor and the homeless found in the Synagogue those who would help them. In the ancient Synagogue, wayfarers and the sick found hostel and hospitality, the orphans their guardians, the mistreated their defenders, the captives their redeemers. No need of the people, no expression of social responsibility failed to find satisfaction in the Synagogue. Historically the Synagogue influenced the Church that followed its pattern of prayer, study and service. The Synagogue today, despite vast changes in the social scene, still serves the needs of the people; as a place of prayer, as a house of study, as the center for fellowship and social welfare, as a source of inspiration to social action.

The Synagogue in Modern Life

The modern Synagogue, also called Temple (both words are equally inadequate in view of the several Hebrew names and functions attached to it), as a place of prayer, holds religious worship on Sabbaths and holidays, and often provides for daily worship. Music and prayer are woven together to form the medium of worship, the prayer book is the guide and compendium for the worshiper. Some of the prayers, some of the music of the Synagogue is as old as the Synagogue. Reflecting the growing and changing need of the people, new prayers and new music have been introduced. Ancient symbols like the Ner Tamid, the perpetual light, and the Menorah, the seven-branched candlestick, are found in the Synagogue, reminding the worshiper of the ceaseless appeal of religious values. Modern practices, like the Confirmation ceremony, represent the response of the Synagogue to the present-day need of reaching the lives of its people. In ancient times, all those who were part of the Jewish community were part of the Synagogue. In modern times, particularly in America, where the Jewish community exists as a group of Jews in a given area, with Jewish institutions which serve them and receive their support, membership in the Synagogue is purely voluntary. The Synagogue is established by and made up of those who choose to be members of its fellowship. More and more in American Jewish life, the Synagogue is emerging as the natural and necessary center of Jewish life and through its voluntary character reaches the largest number of Jews in America. While a Jew may choose not to be a member of a Synagogue, more and more Jews find that their Jewishness has meaning and purpose when they are part of the Synagogue and thus identify themselves as Jews in the best and fullest sense.

The Jewish Home

Another center of activity for Jewish living is the home. Sabbaths and festivals are marked by Jewish home observance. Jewish books, art and ceremonials help to create the Jewish home. The Jewish home is something more than a place where Jews live. The Mezzuzah (small receptacle on

the doorpost containing the prayer beginning "Shema Yisroel—Hear O Israel, the Lord our God, the Lord is One")
suggests that those who enter or leave the house carry with
them the thought of God. The service at the Sabbath or
festival table, in which the mother kindles the Sabbath or
festival candles, the father recites the Kiddush, Sanctification of Sabbath or festival, and the children are blessed,
teaches the beauty of Jewish home life and the importance
of religion in strengthening the ties that bind the family
together. The Seder service at Passover time makes the
family table a place for rehearsing the historic events of
Jewish liberation from ancient slavery, and the need for
securing the blessings of freedom for all people. Joyous
family gatherings, marking Bar Mitzvah and Confirmation,
engagement and marriage, make the Jewish home an important agency in instilling an appreciation of Judaism as
a guide to living. The warmth and welcome of the Jewish
home and Jewish family life are more than memories of
the past, and they stir more than a nostalgia for the scenes
of childhood. The Jewish home gives meaning to Judaism
as it helps to create strength of character and love of the
ideals that add quality to living.

Sabbath and Holidays

The calendar of the Jewish year is marked by a procession of observances that seek through historical reminders
and ceremonial practices to recall and to reinforce the importance of the great ideals of Jewish living. The Sabbath,
beginning on a Friday evening (the day in Jewish practice
begins and ends at sundown) and ending on Saturday
evening, marks the close of each week. As the day of rest
and refreshment of body and spirit, the Sabbath represents
one of the most significant contributions of Judaism to the
moral and social advance of mankind. The Sabbath affirms
that man is not a machine, that man is a child of God, and
as such must have time and opportunity to develop his

God-given nature. It is important that man use this opportunity to enrich his life and to make it more than a time for getting and consuming. Joining with others in Sabbath worship, the Jew discovers his greater and nobler self, finds new strength in the community of interest within the Synagogue, a new feeling that God is with him and that he is with God, as he moves through life. Within the home, the change of pace, the sense of the different and the lovely quality of Sabbath create a mood of relaxation, and offer a release from the pressures and tensions of living in a hectic world. In the story of creation, the Sabbath is spoken of as the time when God the Creator had rest from the labors of creation, and in the Ten Commandments man is enjoined to keep the Sabbath as a day of holiness. Surely, man can make no holier use of the Sabbath than to utilize it as time to recreate his life, to let it reclaim its God-given nature.

The New Year

The calendar of Judaism differs from the secular calendar in a number of ways. It is a lunar calendar and its New Year Day—Rosh Ha-Shono—occurs not on the first day of the first month, but on the first day of the seventh month, Tishri 1, usually in September. In the Bible, the New Year is referred to: "In the seventh month, in the first day of the month, shall be a solemn rest unto you, a memorial proclaimed with the blast of horns, a holy convocation." (Lev. 23:24) It is not a day of hilarious celebration, but a time for sober reflection, a beginning of ten days of solemn consideration of life and its problems, culminating in the Day of Atonement, Yom Kippur. In the Synagogue, the shofar, or ram's horn is sounded, that its ancient call may be heard again as a summons to conscience. Men are called back to God, and the Day of Memorial, Yom Zikaron, or the Day of Blowing the Alarm, Yom Teruah, (other names for the New Year Day) becomes a time for the Jew to begin reclaiming his spiritual heritage as part of a God-serving people. In the home, the New Year is marked by family gathering and reunion. As the family join for the New Year observance, the bread that is broken and blessed at the family table is dipped in honey and eaten with the prayer that the New Year may be a time of sweetness and joy. In the Synagogue and in the home, wherever the Jew meets family and friends he will exchange the greeting, "L'shonoh Tovoh Tikosayvou—Happy New Year—May you be written down for a good year."

The Day of Atonement

The ten days between the New Year and the Day of Atonement are called the Aseres Yemei Teshuvah, Ten Days of Repentance. The Sabbath that occurs during the Ten Days is referred to as Shabbas Shuvah, Sabbath of Return or Repentance, suggesting the goal of the solemn season as a time for man to prepare himself by sincere reflection, by taking account of himself, by self-examination, for a return to the kind of life that may be regarded as worthy in the sight of God and man. The Day of Atonement climaxes the period of serious consideration of the meaning of life, its purpose and the ways in which man may live so as to make the most worthy use of it. The Day of Atonement is a full day given to spiritual reflection within the Synagogue, to prayer, to the contemplation of life and duty. The day is marked by fasting, so that relieved of physical considerations, the individual may give himself completely to spiritual concerns. The Day of Atonement is a time for repentance, for reconciliation of man with himself, his neighbor and his God. The optimism of Judaism expresses itself in the Day of Atonement, in the idea that none are without hope, none are denied the opportunity of self-improvement, that all may approach God with "clean hands and a pure heart," and find Atonement, acceptance before God and encouragement, the strength and power to live a better and happier life. The Synagogue services for the Day of Atonement begin with the Kol Nidre service at the eve of the solemn day. The plaintive Kol Nidre melody is intoned, suggesting man's yearning for God and for forgiveness of sin and error. Judaism calls man to confront sin on the Day of Atonement, not as the inescapable heritage involved in man's weakness, but as the unfortunate result of life not used for its highest purpose. The Day of Atonement urges man to use his powers to turn away from sin, to turn from whatever wrong he may have done, by availing himself of the opportunity of self-correction through repentance. The prayer book holds out this goal of Atonement and urges man to seek it: "Say to them, As I live, saith the Lord God, I have no pleasure in the death of the wicked, but that the wicked turn from his way and live; turn ye, turn ye from your evil ways, for why will ye die, O house of Israel? Have I any pleasure at all that the wicked should die? Saith the Lord God; and not rather that he should return from his ways, and live?"

The Day of Atonement continues with the morning and afternoon services, and includes the opportunity for study and reflection upon the great spiritual treasures contained in the prayer book and in Jewish literature. A special memorial service is included in the Day of Atonement ritual, so that the Congregation, recalling the good and the great of the past, may make the exemplar of their lives an added incentive to self-improvement. The immortality that Judaism teaches is described in the Day of Atonement memorial service as a time when man realizes the deathless character of the goodness that marks men's lives, and its power to remain as a blessing forever. The Neilah, or concluding service, ends the Day of Atonement on a note of hope and spiritual attainment, as the worshipers feel the quickened pulse of a new life opening before them. "Wide open are the gates of Thy forgiveness to all who truly seek to be reconciled with Thee. . . . The shadow which darkens our spirit is vanished; and through the

passing cloud there breaks, with the last rays of the setting
sun, the radiance of Thy forgiving peace."

Sukkos—The Feast of Tabernacles

Sukkos, the Feast of Tabernacles, is celebrated on the
fifteenth day of Tishri, five days after the Day of Atonement. Its origins are very ancient, going back to the time
when the Jews lived as an agricultural people in ancient
Palestine. One of the names for the festival, Chag ho-Osif,
"the Festival of Ingathering," suggests its observance as a
harvest festival. Another of its names, Chag ha-Sukkos, "the
Festival of Booths," by which it is most commonly called,
refers to its double significance as a harvest-time holiday
and as a holiday recalling the time when Israel dwelt in
flimsy booths in the desert. Summarizing its rich and varied
meaning, Sukkos is also called He-chog—"the Festival."
It is a time when the Jew recalls that all men are dependent upon the providence of God, that all must be grateful
for the power of the earth to support and sustain those
who dwell upon it. Thus the Sukkah, symbolic tabernacle,
erected in home and Synagogue, stands as visual reminder
of man's common dependence on God, that what we have
as food and shelter comes not alone from our own labors,
but out of the bounty of God's blessing, through the
natural endowments of earth and water and air. These
blessings are man's to enjoy and to share; given as they
are to all of the children of man, they are to be denied to
none. The Feast of Tabernacles, with its symbols of fruit
and flowers, such as the Esrog, or sweet-smelling citron,
the Lulav, palm branch with myrtle and willow, remind us
not only of our ancient origins as a people, but of our
present duty to share God's blessings, to help His children
everywhere to know the goodness and richness with which
the earth has been endowed. Sukkos is a time of rejoicing,
and as the Jew celebrates the happy festival he is taught

the moral necessity of sharing and laboring, that want and poverty, hunger and suffering may be removed from the experience of men everywhere.

The Sukkos Festival continues for eight days. It concludes with Shemini Atzeres, the Eighth Day of the Festival, and Simchas Torah, the Day of Rejoicing over the Law, suggesting that man's wealth is not limited to material substance, that man's life is dependent upon more than bread. The spirit and mind of man must be nourished as well as his body. When the last chapter of the Torah from the Book of Deuteronomy is read in the Synagogue, the reading of the lessons from the Pentateuch is begun again with the opening chapter of Genesis. The Scrolls of the Law are carried in procession through the Synagogue, so that all, young and old, may realize the importance of Israel's spiritual treasure; God's law—man's moral directive, teaching the way and purpose and value of man's life.

Chanukah—The Feast of Dedication

Arising out of a somewhat later period of Jewish history and experience is the Chanukah Festival or Feast of Dedication. The observance of Chanukah begins on the twenty-fifth day of the month of Kislev, usually during the month of December. The festival recalls the heroism of ancient Israel as it arose in resistance to tyranny and fought for the right of religious liberty. Perhaps it was the first instance in history of a people fighting for freedom of conscience, when the Jews, in 168-165 B.C.E. refused to allow the Graeco-Syrian rulers to impose their pagan cult upon them. Despite the fact that ancient Israel was not a military people, they rebelled against their oppressors. They celebrated their regained freedom by rededicating the Temple at Jerusalem and rekindling the ever-burning lamp. The message of the Chanukah Festival is repeated each year as the candles are lit in home and Synagogue for eight days, and the

Jew is reminded, as indeed the world might well learn, "Not by might, nor by power, but My spirit, saith the Lord of hosts." Chanukah is a time of rejoicing, happy songs are sung, gifts are given and games are played, suggesting that the only happy people is a free people.

Purim—The Feast of Lots

From the Book of Esther in the Bible we derive the observance of Purim, the Feast of Lots. On the eve of the Feast of Lots, the Book of Esther, or Megillah, is read in the Synagogue, reminding the Congregation of the salvation of the ancient Jewish community in Persia, threatened with extinction by Haman, who made his personal dislike into a program of national policy. The Purim festival is celebrated with rejoicing, with parties for children and sending of portions to the poor (*shelach monos*) and the giving of gifts. The Scroll of Esther, in which is given the account of the first Purim, has been the inspiration for numerous Purim plays, for artistic expression and imagery surrounding the Scroll, and for masquerades and carnivals that have come to mark the celebration of the happy holiday.

Pesach—Passover

In the springtime, the great Jewish festival of redemption is observed. Beginning on the eve of the fourteenth day of Nisan, Passover is ushered in with the Seder service, a home service at which the story of the departure from Egypt and the redemption from slavery is recounted. The Passover is a very old observance and represents a combination of a pastoral and historical background that has made the holiday rich in significance and appeal. The Seder service has come to be the chief ceremonial of the Passover. Many Congregations also hold communal celebrations of the Seder for those unable to have the service at home, or in addition to the home observance. The story of the Seder, the epic of the redemption of Israel from ancient slavery, has come to characterize Passover pre-eminently as the Festival of Liberation. Amid songs and prayers, families join together, children ask questions about the meaning of Passover and the father replies, instructing the members of the Seder company in the meaning of the symbols; the unleavened bread, the bitter herbs, the wine, the charoses (sauce with the appearance of mortar), a re-minder of the bricks made by the slaves in ancient Egypt, and the afikomon, the matzoh that is hidden and hunted for by the children to keep their interest alive in the Seder service. The Passover observance is continued for seven days, with services on the first and seventh days in the Synagogue, and with the eating of matzoh, unleavened bread, instead of leavened bread, during the Passover week. The matzoh, referred to as bread of affliction, reminds the Jew that despite his redemption from ancient slavery, man-kind is not yet free, that portions of the world's populace are still victims of the enslavement of fear and bigotry, that many of the children of men are still denied the rights of free men, and are subject to discrimination and restriction. Thus the Passover and the Seder service are observed to call men to engage in the struggle that will bring freedom of body and spirit to men and nations everywhere in the world, that they may, as one humanity under God, be accorded the full and equal rights that are the due of all His children.

Shovuos—The Feast of Weeks

Fifty days after Passover, on the sixth day of the He-brew month Sivan, the Feast of Weeks, Shovuos, is ob-served. The festival has both an agricultural and a his-torical reference to the experience of the Jewish people. The holiday was originally called Chag ha-Kotzir (Ex. 34: 22), the Harvest Feast, or Yom ha-Bikkurim, the Festival

of the First Fruits. In time the observance of Shovuos as
a nature festival faded into forgetfulness and the holiday
came to mark the occasion recorded in the Bible when
Israel received the revelation at Mount Sinai. In the nineteenth century, with the advent of Reform Judaism, Shovuos was made the occasion for Confirmation, when each
new generation of boys and girls might be confirmed in
their faith. The Confirmation ceremony gave new meaning
and importance to the festival that had lost its earlier significance as the people came to be more and more remote
from their earlier and ancient agricultural life. Shovuos is
celebrated in the Synagogue as the time when the revelation of God and His Law becomes the sought-after experience of those who would become part of Jewish life, not
only by birth, but through free and knowing acceptance
as well.

The Jewish Calendar

There are a number of minor observances and fast days
that occur in the Jewish calendar, such as the Fast of Geda-
liah on Tishri 3; Asereth b' Tebes, the tenth of Tebes;
Shivah Asar be' Tammuz, the seventeenth of Tammuz; and
Tisha b' Ab, the ninth of Ab, a fast day marking the destruction of the Temple in Jerusalem. These fast days are no
longer observed by Reform Jews, or for that matter by most
Jews, since the historical reasons for their inauguration
have lost meaning and application in modern life.

The observance of the new moon, Rosh Chodesh, marking the beginning of a new month, is referred to by a special prayer in the prayer book. Lag b'Omer, the thirty-third
day intervening between Passover and the Feast of Weeks,
is said to refer to a time when the scourge of death that
threatened the pupils of Rabbi Akiba came to an end.
Chamishah Asar B' Shevat—the fifteenth day of Shevat, a
New Year of trees—has been revived as a kind of Israel
arbor day, and is sometimes observed as a field day for
children in the religious school.

The Jewish calendar and its corresponding months in the secular calendar is as follows:

Nisan—March or April
   14—Eve of Pesach—Passover
   15—Pesach—Passover—First day
   21—Pesach—Passover—Seventh day

Iyar—April or May

Sivan—May or June
   6—Shovuos—Feast of Weeks

Tammuz—June or July

Ab—July or August

Ellul—August or September

Tishri—September or October
   1—Rosh Ha-shono—New Year Day
   10—Yom Kippur—Day of Atonement
   15—Sukkos—Feast of Tabernacles—First day
   22—Shemini Atzeres—Eighth day of the Feast of Tabernacles

Heshvan—October or November

Kislev—November or December
   25—Chanukah—Feast of Dedication

Tebet—December or January

Shevat—January or February
   15—Chamishah Asar B' Shevat—Fifteenth of Shevat

Adar—February or March
   14—Purim—Feast of Lots

Adar Sheni—Second Adar
   In a leap year, which occurs seven times in a cycle of nineteen years, a second Adar is added and Purim is observed on the fourteenth day of the second Adar.

In ancient times, because the calendar was dependent upon the observance of the appearance of the new moon and the transmission from Palestine of the information that the new month had begun, there was some feeling of uncertainty in communities at a distance from Palestine as to the right day for the observance of holidays, so that a two-day observance was introduced. This custom was continued, and Orthodox Judaism observes the New Year, beginning and conclusion of the Feast of Tabernacles, Passover and Shovuos for two days. Reform Judaism, recognizing the fixed and certain nature of the calendar, has returned to the Biblical observance of the holidays for a single day.

Practices During the Life Cycle of the Jew

From birth to death, there are impressive ceremonials that link the individual to Jewish life. On the eighth day after the birth of a male child (or later if the health of the child requires it) the circumcision ceremony takes place. The mohel, professional circumciser, may perform the ceremony, or the circumcision may be performed by a surgeon, with the rabbi reciting the prayers and conferring the name and blessing upon the child. There is usually present at the circumcision ceremony a small gathering (ten to twenty relatives and friends) which will include the father, who presents his child for circumcision, the Sandek, or godfather, or others who serve in a similar capacity, called Kvater or Kvaterin. The child is usually named after a deceased relative, receiving both a Hebrew and an English name, although the practice is not required nor always followed. As the circumcision is about to be performed, the mohel or rabbi will say: "Praised be Thou, O Lord, our God, Ruler of the world, who hast sanctified us with Thy commandments and enjoined upon us the rite of circumcision." The father of the child will add: "Praised be Thou, O Lord, our God, Ruler of the world, who hast sanctified us with Thy commandments and enjoined us to bring our son into the covenant of Abraham our father." Following the circumcision, the rabbi, in blessing the child will say: "We praise Thee, O Lord, our God, in this hour in which a newborn son has been brought into the covenant of Abraham. May this covenant be fulfilled in him by devotion to Thy law of truth and righteousness, by a marriage worthy of Thy blessing, and by a life enriched with good deeds." The child is then taken to the room of the mother, where a brief prayer for the parents and child is recited.

Naming the Child

At the earliest occasion when the parents of the newborn child can attend the Sabbath services in the Synagogue, a prayer is recited for the naming of the child, whether boy or girl. Marking the occasion of the naming of the child, the parents will customarily make a contribution to the Synagogue, so that acts of benevolence and charity may mark the very beginnings of the life of the child. The ceremony of Pidyan-ha-ben, redemption of the first-born male child, who was regarded as dedicated to the priesthood, has fallen into disuse, and is generally not practiced by Reform Jews, since the priesthood as such is no longer in existence, and the ceremony of redemption would seem to have no application or significance.

The Child at Home

The very young child will soon begin to realize that he is part of a Jewish home. He will find Sabbath candles, kindled by the mother, and the Kiddush recited in Sanctification by the father; he will receive a bit of the Sabbath bread, and the father's hand will rest on his head in bless-

ing, all a delightful and warming experience. He will learn
something of the meaning of Jewishness, and the love and
kindness of family life.

The Child and the Religious School

Even before attending the Religious School, the child
may find in the Jewish nursery school his first introduction
to things Jewish outside of the home. At age six, as he is
enrolled for the beginning of his secular education, he is
taken by his parents to the Religious School. The occasion
of his enrollment in the Religious School is a joyous one.
The child will receive a gift of a book or a sweet or a minia-
ture Torah Scroll, and at a Consecration service in the
Temple, he will receive a blessing from the rabbi. His religious education will be marked by noteworthy events. Bar
or Bas Mitzvah will be the ceremony of introduction into
Jewish life at the age of thirteen for the individual boy or
girl, who is called to the reading of the Torah in the Synagogue. For the class of young people who reach the age of
fifteen to sixteen, there will be the Confirmation ceremony
at Shovuos time, when the Feast of Weeks occurs each
year. These ceremonies have a profound influence upon
the child's life. The Bar or Bas Mitzvah gives the child a
sense of the importance of his Judaism; he feels the personal involvement in the Synagogue, he begins to think of
the Torah, not merely as something out of the Jewish past,
but as containing a lesson and guidance for his own life.
The Confirmation ceremony gives the child a more mature
awareness of his Judaism, a feeling that he is part of the
latest generation, called to know and to practice Judaism.
The Confirmation implants in the child's personality a feeling of identification with noble ideals, a relationship to
Judaism and to Jewish life that is positive and aspiring in
its nature. This relationship enhances the child's life and
stays with him through adult living as a source of strength
of character. The Bar or Bas Mitzvah or Confirmation

should not be regarded as the conclusion of the Jewish education of the individual, or as a kind of graduation from the Religious School. Since Jewish study is a characteristic of Jewish living, the young person and the mature adult are encouraged to continue the process of learning about Judaism, so that the increase of Jewish knowledge may deepen the sense of Jewish consciousness.

Marriage

The Jewish youth is encouraged to seek a Jewish mate. Marriage is regarded as the natural prelude to establishing a Jewish home. Because of the feeling of responsibility on the part of the Jewish people to perpetuate Judaism, intermarriage with non-Jews is not encouraged. Small as is the number of Jews in the world, intermarriage with non-Jews would soon assimilate the Jewish people, and there would be none to carry on the Jewish heritage, to be bearers of Judaism and teachers of its moral law to the world. When intermarriage is contemplated, Reform Judaism offers the opportunity of conversion to Judaism to the non-Jew. A course of preparation in the understanding of Judaism is given by the rabbi, and a ceremony of conversion welcomes the non-Jew into the household of Israel, making him an equal in all respects with the born Jew. (See Chapter V for a discussion of conversion to Judaism and the conversion ceremony.)

Following the engagement of the couple, they will visit the rabbi and consult with him about their forthcoming marriage. Often, on the Sabbath before the wedding, the couple will attend services in the Temple and receive the blessings of the Congregation upon their marriage. The wedding, in accordance with Reform Jewish practice, may take place on any day except the Sabbath, or sacred days of festivals (first and eighth day of Feast of Tabernacles, first and seventh day of Passover, the Feast of Weeks). The wedding may be solemnized in any suitable place, but the

Temple, Temple Chapel, rabbi's study, or the home are
preferred. The wedding ceremony is a simple one, in which
the couple plight their troth, drink from the cup of wine,
recite the ancient formula, "Be thou consecrated unto me
with this ring as my wife (as my husband) according to
the faith of Israel," as the ring or rings are placed on the
finger of bride and groom. The ceremony is concluded as
the rabbi pronounces the threefold priestly benediction
upon the married couple.

Divorced persons may be remarried, and in Reform
Jewish practice the Get, or so-called Jewish divorce, is not
required. Since, in American life the civil authorities grant
the license to marry, Reform Judaism regards the civil divorce as adequate, particularly since the Orthodox requirement of the Get imposes a disability upon the woman,
who can only receive the Get from the man, but cannot
give it to him.

Reform Judaism follows the Biblical list of degrees of
family relationship permissible in marriage and categories
of relationship that are barred from marriage.

Death, Burial and Mourning

As the individual comes to the end of his life, there is a
prayer and service of confession (Viddui) at the deathbed.
The rabbi or others present will recite the declaration of
the unity of God (Shemah) with the dying person if he
is able to speak, or for him if he is not. As the spirit departs
the body the rabbi will declare, "Hear O Israel, the Lord
our God, the Lord is one," affirming the belief in the One-
ness of God at death as at birth.

Judaism does not object to the performance of the
autopsy, or post-mortem examination of the body of the
deceased. It regards the autopsy as a means by which
medical authorities may learn from the dead how to help
the living.

The body of the deceased is as a rule embalmed and prepared for burial on the first or second day after death. The funeral service may be delayed if necessary to await the arrival of relatives of the deceased. The funeral service is conducted by the rabbi, and the burial takes place in the hallowed ground of a Jewish cemetery. After the body is lowered into the grave, the Kaddish prayer, or Sanctification of the Name of God, is recited. Flowers may be placed upon the grave and growing things planted upon it that the memory of the dead may remain forever fresh and lovely in the minds of loved ones.

Following the funeral service, the mourners return to their home. A minyan or service in the home is held, allowing the mourners the opportunity to recite the Kaddish without leaving the home. The mourners remain at home for the week following the funeral, but attend the services in the Synagogue on the Sabbath. Those in mourning for dear ones (father, mother, sister, brother, son, daughter, husband or wife) recite the Kaddish prayer for twelve months after the death of the dear one, and on the anniversary, Yahrzeit, of the death at the services in the Synagogue. In some Synagogues, the whole Congregation rises to recite the Kaddish prayer in memory of all the dead, and in sympathy for the living. When the Kaddish is recited in memory of a dear one, the practice is to do so on the Sabbath following the anniversary date, unless it happens to fall on the Sabbath itself. A tombstone or marker is set upon the grave of the deceased at some time near the first anniversary of the death, and appropriate prayers are recited on the occasion. Contributions in memory of the deceased are made to the Synagogue on the anniversary of the death of a dear one in his memory, and the flowers placed at the pulpit in the Temple may often be placed there in tribute to the memory of the dead.

The custom of visiting the cemetery is not limited to any particular time, although it is not the practice to do so on Sabbaths or holidays. Many Congregations have special memorial services in the cemetery on Memorial Day or on the Sunday between New Year and the Day of Atonement, since it is Jewish practice to visit the cemetery before the New Year or the Day of Atonement.

Marriages, if previously planned, may take place during the month of mourning, and are most simply solemnized. If they have not been previously planned, it is the practice to postpone the wedding celebration until after the thirty days following the death of a dear one, and it may take place at that time even if one is mourning for a mother or father.

Reform Jewish Practice

For guidance in the matter of Reform Jewish practice two volumes on the subject by Rabbi Solomon B. Freehof will be found most helpful. In many Congregations small manuals on Reform Jewish practice compiled by the rabbi are also available.

Prayer and Observance in Daily Life

Judaism does not separate the sacred and the secular. All of life is to be marked by the aspiration for holiness and nobility in living. At home or abroad, at work or play, in business or professional activity, the Jew should be mindful of his God-serving career. Prayer and religious practice in Synagogue and home remind the Jew of this career, help him toward its fulfillment. No joy or achievement in life should go unmarked by the expression of gratitude to God. No sorrow or failure should be without the comfort and encouragement that comes to those who turn to God in prayer. Here are a few of the prayers that may be used in the daily life of the Jew. The *Union Home Prayerbook* (published by the Central Conference of American Rabbis), from which they are taken, contains a complete collection of prayers and meditations for all occasions and experiences in the life of the individual.

Morning Prayer

Bless the Lord, O my soul, and all that is within me, bless His holy Name. I thank Thee Lord, that Thou hast renewed my breath within me this morning, and that my being is awake to the wonders of Thy creation. The heavens declare Thy glory and the firmament showeth Thy handiwork. Help me, O Lord, to make my fellow men sing Thy praises through this day, by being a friend to them, as Thou art my Friend. Let me walk by their side, and enable me to dispel their fears and to relieve their anxieties. May I show them the brightness of goodness, the wonder of love and the power of righteousness; for these gifts come from Thy hands—and I would use them for Thy glory. Amen.

Shemah Yisroel Adonoy Elohaynu Adonoy echod.
Hear, O Israel, The Lord our Cod, the Lord is One.

Morning Prayer for Children

Blessed art Thou, O Lord our God, Father of all, for letting me wake to this new day. O God, be with me always, that I may be loving to my parents and dear ones. Help me to be kind to all. May I willingly obey those who teach me. Lead me in the paths of truth. Help me to be faithful to all my duties.

Shemah Yisroel Adonoy Elohaynu Adonoy echod.
Hear, O Israel, The Lord our God, the Lord is One.
Boruch shem kevode malchuso layolom vo-ed.
Praised be His name, whose glorious kingdom is forever and ever.

Vay-ohavto ays Adonoy Elohechoh bechole lih-vovchoh
oo-vechole nafshechoh oo-vechole may-odechoh.
Thou shalt love the Lord, thy God, with all thy heart,
with all thy soul, and with all thy might.

Night Prayer

O God, as this day closes, humbly I thank Thee for all
that it has brought me; for its joys and also for its trials; for
earnest effort, sweet affection and uplifting hopes.

Grant that my deeds may show that I am worthy of Thy
favor. Strengthen me, O God, that I may love Thee with
all my heart, with all my soul and with all my might. Pardon, O Father, my shortcomings. Help me to forgive all
who may have wronged me; and grant me strength to seek
pardon of all whom I may have offended. O God, Thou who
dost neither sleep nor slumber, spread over me the shelter
of Thy peace, guard my home and all dear to me. Yea, may
the blessings of Thy peace rest upon all Thy children.

Shemah Yisroel Adonoy Elohaynu Adonoy echod.
Hear, O Israel, The Lord our God, the Lord is One.
Boruch shem kevode malchuso layolom vo-ed.
Blessed be His Name, whose glorious Kingdom is for-
ever and ever.
Bi-yohdo afkeed ruchi bih-ays eeshan vih-oh-eeroh.
Vih-im ruchi guh-vee-yohsee, Adonoy lee, vih-lo ee-roh.
I am in Thy care, O God, when I sleep and when I wake.
My body and my soul are thine. Thou art with me, I
will not fear.

Night Prayer for Children

Now the hours of day are over
I thank Thee, Lord, for all Thy good,
For father's care and gentle mother
Who guard and give me daily food.

The quiet stars keep watch above me,
I lay me down to slumber deep.
Guard Thou, O God, all those who love me,
Wake me again from restful sleep.

Shemah Yisroel Adonoy Elohaynu Adonoy echod.
Hear, O Israel, The Lord our God, the Lord is One.
Amen.

Prayer before Eating

Boruch Atoh Adonoy Elohaynu Melech ho-olom hah-
motzee lechem min ho-oretz.
Praised be Thou, O Lord our God, King of the Universe,
who causest the earth to yield food for all.

Prayer for the Sabbath Eve in the Home

Sabbath Eve
Kiddush

*The table is given a festive appearance. A wine cup and
a loaf of bread for the blessing are set before the head of
the household. The ceremony of ushering in the Sabbath
is begun by the kindling of the lights, during which a blessing by the wife is silently asked upon the home and the
dear ones. The following may be used:*

May our home be consecrated, O God, by Thy light.
May it shine upon us all in blessing as the light of love
and truth, the light of peace and goodwill. Amen.

When all are seated, the head of the household says:

Come, let us welcome the Sabbath in joy and peace!
Like a bride, radiant and joyous, comes the Sabbath.
She brings blessings to our hearts; workday thoughts and

cares are put aside. The brightness of the Sabbath light
shines forth to tell that the divine spirit of love abides
within our home. In that light all our blessings are enriched,
all our griefs and trials are softened. At this hour God's
messenger of peace comes and turns the hearts of the parents to the children; and the hearts of the children to the
parents; strengthening the bonds of devotion to that pure
and lofty ideal of the home found in sacred writ.

The head of the household lifts the wine cup and says:

Let us praise God with this symbol of joy and thank
Him for the blessings of the past week, for life, health, and
strength, for home, love, and friendship, for the discipline
of our trials and temptations, for the happiness that has
come to us out of our labors. Thou has ennobled us, O God,
by the blessings of work, and in love and kindness Thou has
sanctified us by the blessings of rest through the commandment: "Six days shalt thou labor and do all thy work, but
the Seventh day is the Sabbath hallowed unto the Lord,
Thy God."

Boruch Atoh Adonoy Elohaynu Melech haolom bo-ray
p'ree hagofen.
Praised be Thou, O Lord our God, King of the Universe,
who has created the fruit of the vine.

*The wine cup is passed around the table and each in
turn drinks from it. The head of the household then breaks
the bread and, dipping a piece of it in salt, pronounces the
blessing:*

Boruch Atoh Adonoy Elohaynu Melech ho-olom hamot-
zee lechem min haoretz.
Praised be Thou, O Lord our God, King of the Universe,
who causest the earth to yield food for all.

Each one at the table likewise partakes of bread and salt. Then the parent, with hands upon the head of each child in turn, silently pronounces such a blessing as the heart may prompt, or uses the following formula:

May the God of our fathers bless you. May He who has guided us unto this day lead you to be an honor to our family. May He who has protected us from all evil make you a blessing to Israel and to all mankind. Amen.

Celebration of Chanukah

Chanukah, or Feast of Dedication, lasts eight days. On the first evening one light is kindled, the number of lights being increased by one on each successive evening. Before the kindling of the lights, the following is said:

Boruch Atoh Adonoy Elohaynu Melech ho-olom asher kid-shonu bihmitzvo-sove vih-ztivonu lih-hadleek ner shel Chanukah.
Praised be Thou, O Lord our God, Ruler of the world who hast sanctified us by Thy commandments, and bidden us kindle the Chanukah lights.

Boruch Atoh Adonoy Elohaynu Melech ho-olom she-oso nisim lah-avosaynu bahyomim ho-haym baz-man hazeh.
Praised be Thou, O Lord our God, Ruler of the world, who wonderfully helped our fathers at this season in days of yore.

Boruch Atoh Adonoy Elohaynu Melech ho-olom sheh-cheh-he-yo-no vih-kee-yih-monu vih-hig-ee-onu lazman hazeh.
Praised be Thou, O Lord our God, Ruler of the World, who hast granted us life, sustained us and permitted us to celebrate this joyous festival.

After kindling the lights, say the following:

Praised be Thou, O Lord our God, King of the Universe, for the inspiring truths of which we are reminded by these Chanukah lights.

We kindle them to recall the great and wonderful deeds wrought through the zeal with which God filled the hearts of the heroic Maccabees. These lights remind us that we should ever look unto God whence comes our help.

As their brightness increases from night to night, let us more fervently give praise to God for the ever-present help He has been to our fathers in the gloomy nights of oppression and trouble.

The sages and heroes of all generations made every sacrifice to keep the light of God's truth burning brightly. May we and our children be inspired by their example: so that at last, Israel may be a guide to all men on the way of righteousness and peace.

Chanukah Song

(Music in the *Union Hymnal*)

Rock of Ages, let our song
Praise Thy saving power;
Thou, amidst the raging foes,
Wast our sheltering tower.
Furious, they assailed us,
But Thine arm availed us;
And Thy word
Broke their sword
When our own strength failed us.

Kindling new the holy lamps
Priests approved in suffering,
Purified the nation's shrine,
Brought to God their offering,
And His courts surrounding
Hear, in joy abounding,
Happy throngs
Singing songs
With a mighty sounding.

Children of the Martyr-race,
Whether free or fettered,
Wake the echoes of the songs
Where ye may be scattered!
Yours the message cheering,
That the time is nearing
Which will see
All men free,
Tyrants disappearing.

Birthday Celebration

O Eternal God, Thou art the master of our destiny
and the source of all life. Our times are in Thy hand.
We thank Thee day by day for Thy manifold blessings
and, as year follows year, we are grateful that Thou has
sustained us.

We gather today in special joy and thankfulness to
share in the happiness of our dear .... It is Thou
who hast granted him (her) strength and life. Bless him
(her), O Lord, with health and joy. Sustain him (her) in
times of sickness and console him (her) in days of sorrow. Endow him (her) with long life and abundance of
blessing: and grant to us the joy of meeting, for many

years, as on this day, a loving family in mutual reverence
and unbroken unity.

Boruch Atoh Adonoy Elohaynu Melech ho-olom sheh-
cheh-he-yo-no, vih-kee-yih-monu vih-hig-eeonu lazman
hazeh.
Praised be Thou, O Lord, our God, who hast kept us in
life, sustained us and brought us to this happy day.

Boruch Atoh Adonoy Elohaynu Melech ha-olom hah-
motze lechem min haoretz.
Praised be Thou, O Lord our God, ruler of the world,
who causest the earth to yield food for all.

Family Yahrzeit Light Ceremonial

*The family is gathered at dusk, before the evening meal,
on the eve of the anniversary of the death of the departed.
The head of the family speaks:*
Dear ones—at this moment which bears the memory
of our beloved ———, let us join hands in token of God's
grace. A link has been broken in the chain of affection
which has long bound us together, yet the blessed bonds
of home and love remain. With prayerful hearts, we
receive this divine gift of life which holds us together
in family union.
Eternal God, we thank Thee that in the hour of be-
reavement Thou didst sustain us. Though sorrow lingers
in our memory, we have learned that love is stronger
than death. At Thy command, our loved one has gone
to his (her) eternal rest. To Thee we lift grateful hearts,
for we sense our beloved in our very midst as a living
presence. We acknowledge Thy mercy, O Father, who
doth strengthen Thy Children with faith and peace.

*At this point it would be appropriate for members of the
group to recite a passage from the Bible or prayer book*

which was a favorite of the departed, or to recall intimate characteristics and tender incidents in his or her life.

As our dear one lives again for us in these words and memories, we kindle the Yahrzeit light and sanctify it in the remembrance of the divine word: "The spirit of man is the candle of the Lord."

Kindle the light.

Zecher tsadik liv-rocho. The memory of the righteous is a blessing.

IV — The Organization of Jewish Life in America

The American Jewish community, a term loosely used to describe the totality of Jew and Judaism in America, consists of some five and a half million Jews. Jews live in all parts of the United States, with a preponderance of their number to be found in large cities. Almost half of the total Jewish population is to be found in the metropolitan area of New York City. Yet there are hundreds of Jewish communities in the United States, ranging from less than a hundred to ten thousand. There are many towns and small cities in which only one to a score of Jewish families will be found. In every community having a Jewish population, and often in those with only ten or twelve families, a Synagogue will be found. In many Synagogues in the smaller communities, laymen will serve as leaders in worship, and as teachers of the children. In larger communities there will be more than one Synagogue, with the rabbi as spiritual leader, and in cases of larger Synagogues, more than one rabbi will serve the Congregation. In addition there may be a cantor, a director of religious education, a Hebrew teacher, and many part-time voluntary or professional religious school teachers as part of the staff of the Synagogue. As auxiliaries to the Synagogue there are a number of organizations such as a Sisterhood or Women's Guild, Brotherhood or Men's Club, Youth Groups, Parent-Teacher Associations, Young Married Group, Adult Study Groups. A Board of Trustees and officers of the Congregation direct the affairs of the Synagogue with the rabbi as spiritual leader. Numerous committees are responsible for the several functions of the Synagogue. Many and varied activities for the benefit of its membership and community are carried on by the Synagogue and its organizations in addition to religious services and religious education. These activities may serve the social, philanthropic, social welfare, social action and civic improvement interests of the community. Since the Synagogue seeks to influence the whole of life, it considers nothing human alien to its concern.

While the Synagogue in America is a completely independent institution, and the individual congregation a completely autonomous unit, there are a number of national and regional organizations of Synagogues that have banded together the local Synagogues for mutual benefit and for the advancement of their common interests. The Union of American Hebrew Congregations, the oldest of the national Synagogue institutions, embraces some 550 of the Reform, Liberal, Progressive Congregations in the United States, Canada and related areas. It has a number of regional organizations, such as the New York Federation of Reform Synagogues, composed of and serving Congregations in metropolitan New York and similar Federations of Congregations in other metropolitan centers, and like the New Jersey Council of the Union, composed of and serving Congregations in one or more states. The national body of the Conservative Congregations in the United States is the United Synagogue of America, and one of the Orthodox national Synagogue bodies is known as Union of Orthodox Jewish Congregations. A national body like the Union of American Hebrew Congregations is responsible for many activities and departments. It is the sponsoring and patron body of the Hebrew Union College—Jewish Institute of Religion, a school for the training of rabbis, cantors and educators. The Commission on Jewish Education of the Union of American Hebrew Congregations provides for the production of educational materials, curricula and teacher-training programs for its member Congregations and for many other Congregations that make use of its materials and guidance.

The Department of Synagogue Activities advises the local Congregations on all aspects of the Synagogue program and administration and provides information and guidance to Social Action Committees. The Commission on Public Information about Judaism distributes material providing general information about Judaism and the Union publishes a magazine, *American Judaism,* which is sent to 200,000 families belonging to its local Congregations. The Department of New Congregations aids and guides groups in the formation of new Congregations. The National Federation of Temple Sisterhoods, the National Federation of Temple Brotherhoods, the National Federation of Temple Youth representing groups in the local Synagogues are affiliates of the Union of American Hebrew Congregations. Likewise affiliated with the national body are the National Association of Temple Secretaries and National Association of Temple Educators, Associations of men and women professionally engaged in the local Synagogue.

In addition to the Synagogue there may be other Jewish institutions in the local community. The Jewish Community Center or Young Men's and Women's Hebrew Association (the former name is the more common one) is found in many medium-size and large Jewish communities. Its purpose will be to provide a central meeting place and to sponsor social, athletic and cultural programs for the youth. It will include in its program: clubs, forums and lectures series for older men and women as well as for the children and young people of the community. The Community Center is supported by membership fees and grants from the local Jewish Welfare Fund, and at times by grants from the general Welfare Federation fund of the community. The Community Center has a local governing board and is part of the national body known as the Jewish Welfare Board, which also serves young men and women in the armed forces.

The local Jewish Welfare Fund raises funds annually through voluntary contributions from the whole community for the support of a variety of Jewish organizations and agencies, local, national and overseas. Chief among the beneficiaries of such funds will be the United Jewish Appeal, which provides support for relief and rehabilitation activities for Jews in many lands outside of the United States, furnishing aid to immigrants to Israel and to projects in the State of Israel that contribute to the sustenance and eventual independence of its settlers. Many other institutions are supported by the local community; Jewish hospitals, Jewish child care associations, Jewish family services, homes for the Jewish aged and chronically ill, bureaus of Jewish education, and Jewish community councils.

National institutions and organizations such as the Zionist Organization of America, the American Jewish Congress, the American Jewish Committee, B'nai B'rith, Hadassah, Council of Jewish Women, have local chapters that carry on programs co-ordinate with the national bodies. In larger Jewish communities these organizations may be fairly numerous as they relate the local community to the national program and seek support for it. Many of these organizations, like the Zionist Organization, Hadassah, Jewish National Fund, American Fund for Israel Institutions, provide support for a variety of projects and interests in the State of Israel. Others, like the American Jewish Congress, the American Jewish Committee, the Anti-Defamation League of B'nai B'rith, the Jewish Labor Committee, seek to serve the American Jewish community and promote activities in defense of the rights of Jews, for the better understanding of Jews and Judaism and for the social and civil advancement of the American community as a whole. There are also national institutions such as the Jewish National Home for Asthmatic Children at Denver, the Leo N. Levi Memorial Hospital at Hot Springs, United HIAS, Service for Aid to Immigrants, the Jewish Publication Society, American Ort Federation for Rehabilitation through training, American Jewish Historical Society and many others that serve a variety of cultural, educational, social service and welfare needs of the Jewish community. The *American Jewish Yearbook* lists more than two hundred such organizations.

Many Jewish communities have an Anglo-Jewish periodical, issued, as a rule, weekly, that carries news and articles about Jewish affairs, local and national. These periodicals are usually published as private ventures, although on occasion they may be supported by a local agency like the Jewish Welfare Fund.

On college and university campuses the Jewish student organization is the Hillel Foundation, maintained by B'nai B'rith and grants from local Jewish Welfare Funds. The Hillel Foundation provides a program of religious, cultural and social activity for Jewish students and is usually under the direction of a rabbi. Many colleges and universities will have specifically Jewish fraternities and sororities, most of which are local chapters of national fraternities and which bear Greek letter names such as Sigma Alpha Mu or Zeta Beta Tau.

The Jewish Community

As we see this picture of the Jewish community, it may appear as no more than a collection of organizations, institutions and activities in which Jews participate and to which Jews give support. While the Jewish community may have no organic character, nor does it seek to set the Jew apart from the general community and its interests, it does have a historical background and does command the interest of a majority of Jews who constitute it. Through the centuries of Jewish life in Asia, Africa and Europe, when there were no publicly supported institutions for social welfare, Jewish care for the needy, the sick, the orphaned and the oppressed was well organized and accepted as a moral responsibility for the Jewish community.

The Synagogue as a Bes-ha-Keneses was a social center in the best and truest sense. A man who was wronged could interrupt the worship of the Congregation to demand recognition of his complaint. If danger threatened the Jews, they assembled in the Synagogue to take counsel with one another as to how to ward it off or to meet it when it assaulted them. Jewish communities were known to have impoverished themselves to ransom fellow Jews who were about to be sold into slavery. When the Revolutionary War in America was hard-pressed for funds to carry on, Haym Solomon is reputed to have sent messages to the then existing Synagogues appealing for money to be loaned to the cause of American liberty. On many occasions, the Synagogue was the scene of mass gatherings of Jews who protested against the violation of human rights, against the oppression of the Czars and the terror of a Hitler. Underlying the Jewish community and giving it meaning is a sense of religious involvement, a feeling of moral commitment. The Jewish community is an instrument permitting the individual Jew to express himself Jewishly, not alone in the philanthropic sense but as a positive demonstration that the Jew has a contribution to make toward the advancement of society and civilization.

V — Conversion to Judaism

In present-day Judaism there are no missionaries, nor is there an active missionary movement seeking to win converts to Judaism. Yet Judaism welcomes all who come freely; sincerely and knowingly desire to become Jews. Since both the Jewish people and Judaism have a long history, covering more than three thousand years, there are historical reasons that explain this situation.

The Bible makes reference to those who joined the household of Israel in the most ancient times. The Hebrew word *"ger,"* translated "stranger," used frequently in the Bible, is generally taken to refer to those who were not born in the household of Israel, but joined it out of choice. An entire book of the Bible—Ruth—tells the story of that ancestress of King David, who declared her acceptance of Judaism in the immortal words:

> And Ruth said: "Entreat me not to leave thee and to return from following after thee; for whither thou goest, I will go; and where thou lodgest, I will lodge; thy people shall be my people, and thy God my God; where thou diest, will I die, and there will I be buried; the Lord do so to me, and more also, if aught but death part thee and me." (I:16,17)

In post-Biblical Jewish literature, we find numerous references to those who joined themselves to the household of Israel, indicating that it was not uncommon. Expressive of the general interest in and attitude toward converts are statements in rabbinic literature:

Thus taught the sages in the Mishnah: When a convert comes to be converted, we stretch out the hand to bring him beneath the wings of the Shekinah (Divine Presence).

"Dear are converts, for every term that is applied to Israel (in the Bible) is applied also to converts," i.e., such terms as servants, ministers, friends, priests, as well as such concepts as covenant, favor, protection, are used Biblically for both native and converted Jews. Moreover, Abraham and David applied to themselves the term "ger" (convert). (Quoted by Rabbi Bernard J. Bamberger in *Proselytism in the Talmudic Period.*)

Some converts to Judaism became very famous as scholars and teachers—Aquila, who translated the Bible into Greek; Onkelos, who wrote the Aramaic translation and commentary of the Bible. A number of rabbis are referred to as converts to Judaism and others were children of converts as may be gathered from the name Rabbi Judah ben Gerim (son of converts).

In the Roman period, even after Judea had been conquered by the military might of Rome, there were those who rejected paganism and sought in Judaism a living, moral and meaningful faith. In his *History of the Jews,* Graetz makes reference to this when he writes: "It is an extraordinary fact that during the half century after the destruction of the Jewish state, there were everywhere conversions to Judaism, both in the East and in Asia Minor, but especially in Rome." (Volume 2, Chapter 14, page 383). Among these converts were famous personages, like Queen Helen of Adiabne, her sons Izates and Monabaz, Flavius Clemens, Roman senator and consul, and Fulvia, wife of Saturnius, a Roman senator. One woman, Beluria, a convert to Judaism, is referred to as "Mater Synagogarum, mother of the synagogue."

When religions became instruments of governments,

Christianity in Rome in the fourth century, Mohammedanism in the Arabic nations in the seventh century, and the
armed might of the state was used to force men and women
to become converts to the religion of the state, Jews ceased
to encourage converts to Judaism and were in fact prevented from doing so by the edicts of the government
(Graetz, *History of the Jews*, Volume 2, page 562, Volume 3,
pages 87-88). Yet, even during the dark centuries of the
Middle Ages, when persecution was visited upon Jews in
almost every land where they dwelt, there were those who
were attracted to Judaism. Some of these joined the household of Israel, despite the threat of persecution and, like
Count Valentin Potocki, in seventeenth-century Poland, became martyrs for their newfound faith.

In modern times, when men and women everywhere are
disturbed by the paganism rampant in the world and the
materialism that threatens it, they turn again to this ancient
faith of Judaism, seeking in its teachings a way of life that
can give them hope for the future. Some of these men and
women have had no religion. They have been disillusioned
by the failure of science to provide the world with security
or with political and social philosophies, that have promised
but not produced an orderly, peaceful world. They come
to Judaism and seek in its teachings of the fatherhood of
God, the brotherhood of man, in its ideals of social morality
and justice, an outlook upon life, a way of living that has
meaning and validity. Men and women, contemplating
marriage and the necessity of establishing a home and
rearing children have suddenly found themselves forced
to the realization that without a means of faith in the future,
they are likely to find themselves lost and frightened in a
world they never made; without direction and destiny, in
a world they should have a hand in fashioning. Many of
these men and women now ask the question:

CAN ANYONE BECOME A JEW? The answer is "Yes—anyone who desires to learn the meaning of Judaism and to live

according to the teachings of Judaism." Birth, nationality, economic condition, former belief or nonbelief bar none from entering the household of Israel.

HOW DOES ONE GO ABOUT BECOMING A JEW? Seek out and confer with the rabbi of a Jewish congregation. (Information about the rabbi in your community can be secured by calling or writing to the Union of American Hebrew Congregations, 838 Fifth Avenue, New York City 21, REgent 7-8200.) The rabbi is a teacher of Judaism. As the spiritual leader of the Congregation, his primary purpose is to teach the meaning of Judaism to his Congregation. He is also interested in helping anyone understand the meaning of Judaism. In asking for information, no one will be obligated or committed to go beyond the search for knowledge and guidance. After having discussed his interest in Judaism with the rabbi, if the individual wishes to acquire a fuller knowledge of Judaism, the rabbi will make it possible for him to pursue a course of studies. In New York City, under the auspices of the New York Federation of Reform Synagogues and the Association of Reform Rabbis of New York, there is a continuing course for the preparation of prospective converts to Judaism. There are similar courses in Chicago, Los Angeles and Philadelphia. In other communities, the rabbi will arrange for individual instruction.

WHAT IS TAUGHT IN THE COURSE OF STUDY ABOUT JUDAISM? Something of the history of the Jews and Judaism, the basic concepts of Judaism concerning God, Israel, mankind, the Torah, the moral law and ethical ideals are taught. An introduction to the literature, rituals, practices and prayers of Judaism is given. Some understanding of the place and function of the Synagogue in Jewish life, of the present-day organizations within the Jewish community, and of the cultural interests and philanthropic undertakings of Jews who seek actively to express their Judaism by contributing to the welfare of fellow Jews and the advancement of humanity, is presented. In the initial course of instruction, the individual will not learn all there is to know about the vast life and lore and teachings of Judaism. All Jews should continue the study of Judaism throughout their lifetime, for study is regarded not only as a means of increasing the knowledge and meaning of religion, but also as an incentive to apply its values in influencing the daily conduct of life.

THE CEREMONY OF CONVERSION TO JUDAISM. Upon completion of the initial course of study, the rabbi will plan a ceremony of conversion which usually takes place in the Synagogue (but not usually as part of public worship) in the presence of several witnesses, other rabbis and leaders of the congregation. In the ceremony, the convert to Judaism is welcomed into the household of Israel. He or she will be asked to share in the faith and fate of the Jewish people, to promise to lead a Jewish life and to pledge that he or she will rear any children that he may have as Jews. He or she will be given an additional Biblical name as symbol and reminder of the acceptance of Judaism and a certificate as an official record of the event. A duplicate of the certificate will be placed in the archives of the congregation.

Note: Reform Judaism does not require circumcision or ritual bath of converts to Judaism. Orthodox and Conservative Judaism make these requirements.

WILL THE CONVERT TO JUDAISM BE THE SAME AS ANY OTHER JEW? He will be in every way, having the same opportunities and the same responsibilities. He will be asked to affiliate with the Synagogue, make his home a Jewish home and little sanctuary of the Jewish spirit, teach his children the meaning and practice of Judaism, work with fellow Jews for the understanding and application of the ideals of Judaism, seek to advance the welfare of the community in which he lives, practice philanthropy, aiding Jews and Jewish institutions everywhere, serving the cause of humanity and promoting the peace of the world. He or

she may marry another Jew or Jewess without restriction
and in accordance with the usual practices of Judaism concerning marriage. Rabbi Solomon B. Freehof in his book
on *Reform Jewish Practice* points out: "Both traditional
and Reform Judaism consider the marriage between a Jew
and a convert to Judaism as full Jewish marriage."

VI — A Vocabulary of Terms of Jewish Interest and Usage

Adas. Congregation of.

Afikomon. Literally, dessert. Piece of matzoh hidden at the beginning of the Seder service. Children hunt for the afikomon at the end of the meal and receive a reward for finding it.

Alef Bes. Hebrew Alphabet—20 consonants, 5 final letters, 7 vowels.

Aron Hakodesh. Holy Ark in the Synagogue in which the Torah or Scrolls of the Law are kept.

Aseres ha Dibros. Ten Commandments.

Ashkenazic. Referring to usage among Jews of Central and Eastern European origins.

Bar Mitzvah, Bas Mitzvah. The ceremony (also the name for the individual involved) at which a boy, or a girl, at the age of thirteen, after adequate study, accepts Judaism and assumes the religious responsibilities of being a Jew.

Baruch. Blessed.

Berocha. Blessing.

Bes Am. House of the People, one of the oldest terms to describe the Synagogue.

Bes Ha Keneses. House of Gathering (one of the names used to describe the Synagogue).

Bes Ha Midrash. House of Study (also one of the descriptions of the Synagogue).

Bes Ha Tefiloh. House of Prayer (another description for the Synagogue).

Bes Hamikdosh. The Holy Temple—referring to the Temple that stood in Jerusalem. "Mikdosh" means sanctuary.

Bimah. Pulpit (may also refer to the raised platform from which the Torah is read in the Synagogue).

Bris Milah. Rite of circumcision.

Brith. Covenant into which Jewish male children are ushered through the rite of circumcision. Used also to refer to the moral covenant between God and Israel.

B'sommim. Spices, used during Havdalah ceremony.

Challah. Twisted loaf of bread used on the Sabbath and holidays.

Chamishah Asar B'Shevat. The fifteenth day of the Hebrew month of Shevat. A minor festival known as the New Year of the Trees—Jewish Arbor Day.

Chanukah. Feast of Dedication or Lights.

Chayim, L'chayim. Used as a toast—"To life"; sometimes L'chayim tovim, "good life."

Chazan. Cantor.

Choson. Bridegroom.

Chumosh. Pentateuch—first five books of the Bible.

Chupa. Bridal Canopy.

Dreydel. Top used at Chanukah time.

Eretz Yisroel. Land of Israel.

Esrog. Citron (one of the fruits displayed during the Feast of Tabernacles).

Etz Chayim. Tree of Life (a metaphor used in referring to the Torah or the name given to the staves on which the Torah is bound).

Gemarah. Interpretation of the Mishnah.

Get. Bill of divorcement.

Gut Yom Tov. A good holiday.

Haftarah. The selection from the prophetical writings, read in the Synagogue after the reading of the Torah.

Hag Somayach. A happy holiday. A greeting used on holidays.

Haggadah. Ritual for the Passover service in the home. May also refer to Hebrew literature of an ethical nature.

Havdalah. Ceremony marking the conclusion of the Sabbath.

Kaddish. Prayer in sanctification of God. Although recited by mourners it is not a prayer for the dead.

Kallah. Bride. May also refer to a conference for Jewish learning.

Kehillah. Term used to describe a Jewish communal organization. Sometimes used to denote a Congregation.

Kesubah. A written document. Usually in reference to the marriage contract.

Kesubim. Holy writings. Third section of the Bible.

Kiddush. Ceremony for the sanctification of Sabbath or festival. Also refers to the wine used during the ceremony.

Kodosh. Holy.

Kohen. Priest.

Kosher. Fit or proper. Prepared according to Jewish ritual requirements.

Lag b' Omer. A minor festival commemorating the end of an epidemic affecting the disciples of Akiba.

Leviyah. Funeral.

L'Shonah Tovah. For a good year, or Happy New Year.

Lulav. Palm branch to which are bound the myrtle (hadas) and willow (arovoh) leaves used during Sukkos, Feast of Tabernacles.

Machsur. Holiday prayer book.

Matzoh. Unleavened bread.

Mazel Tove. Good luck or congratulations.

Megillah. Scroll—usually refers to Scroll or Book of Esther in the Bible. Books of Ruth, Lamentations, Song of Songs and Ecclesiastes are also referred to as "Megillos."

Mezzuzah. Small metal, wooden or plastic box containing a parchment scroll, attached to right-hand doorpost. It contains the prayer beginning with the "Shema—Hear, O Israel!"

Minyon. Congregation of ten persons gathered for worship.

Mishnah. Collection of rabbinical interpretations.

Mogen Dovid. Star of David.

Motzi. Blessing over bread. Used as grace before meals.

M'lamed. Teacher.

Ner Tamid. Eternal Light.

Neviim. Prophets (second section of the Bible).

Nigun. Tune. Used to refer to Synagogue melodies.

Oneg Shabbot. Literal meaning "Joy of the Sabbath." Usually refers to the Sabbath reception.

Parnas. Leader of the Congregation.

Perashah. Weekly section of reading from the Torah.

Peroches. Curtain before the Ark where the Torah is kept.

Pesach. Passover.

Purim. Feast of Lots, or Feast of Esther.

Rosh Ha-shono. New Year. Literally, "Head of the Year."

Seder. Ritual supper which ushers in Pesach (the word literally means "order," for order of the service).

Sefer Torah. Book or Scroll of the Law.

Sephardic. Referring to usage among Jews of Spanish or Portuguese origins.

Shabbat Sholom. Sabbath peace.

Shabbas. Sabbath.

Shalach-monos. Sending of gifts—Purim gifts.

Shema. First word of the Hebrew prayer declaring the unity of God.

Shemini Atzeres. Eighth day of the Feast of Weeks, the concluding day of the Feast of Tabernacles.

Shochet. The person who slaughters cattle and poultry for human consumption, in accordance with Jewish law.

Shofar. Ram's horn, sounded at New Year Day services and at close of Day of Atonement services.

Sholom, Sholom Alaychem. Peace be unto you—greeting and farewell.

Shamash. Ninth candle used to kindle the other eight candles ot the Chanukah Menorah. Literally "servant." Custodian ot the Synagogue.

Shovuos. Feast of Weeks.

Siddur. Prayer book.

Sidrah. Section of the Torah read each week in the Synagogue.

Simcha. Occasion of joy.

Simchas Torah. Rejoicing over the law.

Smicha. Ordination (literally, "laying on of the hands," which is the Biblical method of consecrating a leader).

Sukkos. Feast of Tabernacles.

Suko. Enclosure bedecked with fruit, leaves. Reminiscent of the fragile dwellings in which the Israelites lodged during their forty years in the wilderness.

Talmud. Collection of rabbinical writings including the Mishnah and the Gemarah.

Talmud Torah. Hebrew School (literally, the study of the Torah, study of the law).

Talis. Prayer shawl.

Tefilo. Prayer.

Tenach. A Hebrew word for Bible—from the first letters of the three parts of the Bible: Torah (Law), Neviim (Prophets) and Kesubim (Holy Writings).

Terayfah. Torn or unfit, not proper—according to Dietary Laws.

T'filin. Phylacteries.

Torah. Scroll of the Law. Used as a word referring to all of Jewish knowledge.

Yad. Hand or pointer used in reading from the Torah.

Yahrzeit. Anniversary of the death of a dear one.

Yerushalyim. Jerusalem.

Yeshiva. School of higher Jewish learning.

Yisroel. Israel—name originally given to patriarch Jacob—used to refer to people of Israel—also to State of Israel.

Yom Kippur. Day of Atonement.

Yom Tov. Holyday (literally, good day).

Zedakah. Charity.

Note: In the transliteration of Hebrew words, the usage may vary according to the Ashkenazic (Western or German) or Sephardic (Eastern or Spanish) pronunciation of Hebrew letters. Thus we may find "Adath" as well as "Adas" for "Congregation of" "Beth" as well as "Bes" for "House of," "Boruch" as well as "Baruch" for "Blessed" and so forth. The most commonly used forms are given above.

VII — Reading List

History

Baron—*A Social and Religious History of the Jews*
Graetz—*History of the Jews,* 6 vols.
Learsi—*The Jew in America: A History*
Levinger—*A History of the Jews in the United States*
Margolis and Marx—*A History of the Jewish People*
Orlinsky—*Ancient Israel*
Roth—*Bird's-Eye View of Jewish History*
Sachar—*History of the Jews*

Bible

The Holy Scriptures
Freehof—*Preface to Scriptures*
Cohen—*Pathways Through the Bible*

Beliefs

Baeck—*The Essence of Judaism*
Bamberger—*The Story of Judaism*
Bernstein—*What the Jews Believe*
Cohon—*Judaism—A Way of Life*
Cohon—*What We Jews Believe*
Kertzer—*What Is a Jew?*
Kohler—*Jewish Theology*
Moore—*Judaism in the First Centuries of the Christian Era,* 3 vols.
Silver—*Where Judaism Differed*

Prayer and Prayer Books

The Union Prayerbook, Volumes 1 and 2
Dembitz—*Jewish Services in Synagogue and Home*
Freehof—*The Small Sanctuary*

Customs, Practices and Ceremonies
   Idelsohn—*The Ceremonies of Judaism*
   Markowitz—*Leading a Jewish Life in the Modern World*
   Schauss—*The Jewish Festivals*
   ———*Lifetime of a Jew*

Jewish Encyclopedias
   The Jewish Encyclopedia
   The Universal Jewish Encyclopedia

Reform Judaism
   Freehof—*Reform Jewish Practice*, Volumes 1 and 2
   Philipson—*The Reform Movement in Judaism*
   Schwartzman—*Reform Judaism in the Making*

Literature
   Cohen—*Everyman's Talmud*
   Feuer and Eisenberg—*Jewish Literature Since the Bible*,
      Books 1 and 2
   Ginzberg—*The Legends of the Jew*, 7 vols.
   Runes—*The Wisdom of the Torah*
   Schwarz—*The Jewish Caravan*
   Waxman—*A History of Jewish Literature*

American Jewish Community
   The American Jewish Yearbook, Volumes 1-58

Index

A

Abraham, 1, 3, 4, 81
Abraham ibn Ezra, 18
Adler, Samuel, 40
Alexander the Great, 10
Alexandria, 10
American Jewish Committee, 99
American Jewish Congress, 99
American Jewish Historical Society, 99
American Jewish Yearbook, 100
American Ort Federation for Rehabilitation Through Training, 99
Amoraim, 13
Amos, 5
Ashkenazic, 112
Anglo-Jewish Periodicals, 100
Aquila, 103
Australia, 48
Antiochus Epiphanes, 10
autopsy, 84
Anti-Semitism, 34, 40, 41, 44
Arab, Arabic, 18, 43, 46, 47, 104
Arab League, 46
assimulation, 9
Assyria, Assyrians, 4, 5
Azariah dei Rossi, 25

B

Baal, Baalim, 2, 3, 4
Babylonia, Babylonian, 7, 15, 66
Bachya ibn Pakuda, 18
Bamberger, Bernard J., 103
Beluria, 103
Benjamin of Tudela, 18
Baeck, Leo, 58
Balfour Declaration, 43
Bar Mitzvah, 70, 82
Bes Am—House of The People, 8, 9, 66

Bes-ha-Keneses—House of Gathering, 68, 100
Bes-ha-Midrash—House of Study, 67
Bes-ha-Tefiloh—House of Prayer, 66
Bible, 10, 16, 23
Bnai Brith, 99
Brandeis, Louis D., 43
Bulan, King of the Khazars, 17
Burial, 85

C

Cabbalah, Cabbalists, 23, 24
Calendar, Jewish, 78 ff.
Canaan, 1, 2
Caro, Joseph, 25
Central Conference of American Rabbis, 40
Chanukah, Feast of Dedication, 10, 75 ff, 91 ff
Charleston, South Carolina, 37, 38
Chassidim, Chassidism, 27, 28, 29
Chassidism, Habad School of, 29
Chicago, 105
Chmielnicki, Bogdan, 26
Christian, Christians, Christianity, 12, 20, 21, 22, 30, 32, 104
Circumcision, 80 ff
Columbus, 21
Communism, Communists, 44
Comité des Délégations Juives, 43
Community, American Jewish, 96 ff
Confirmation, 70, 89, 82
Congregation, 96 ff
Congregation Beth Elohim, Charleston, So. Carolina, 39
Congregation Emanu-El, New York City, 39
Congregation Har Sinai, Baltimore, Maryland, 39
Congregation Keneseth Israel, Philadelphia, 39
Congregation Shearith Israel, 37

Conservative Judaism, 41, 48, 106
Conversion, 83, 102 ff
Converts, 14, 21, 102 ff
Courses for Converts, 105
Crusades, 18, 19, 20
Cossack, 26
Cyrus, King, 8

D

Daas Elohim—Knowledge of God, 50, 56
David, King, 2, 3
Day of Atonement, 71 ff
Derishat Zion—The Quest For Zion, 42
Desecrating the Host, 20
Deuteronomy, 6, 7
Diaspora, 13
Divorce, 84
Don Joseph Nasi, 25
Donna Grazia Mendesia, 25
Dreyfus, Alfred, 41
Dubno, Solomon, 32
Dutch, 31, 36
Dutch West Indies Company, 36
Duties of the Heart, 18

E

Education, 56, 57
Education, Jewish, 48, 56, 97
Education, religious, 56
Egypt, 2, 7
Einhorn, David, 40
Elias de Medigo, 25
Elias Levita, 25
Eliot, George, 42
Emancipation, 34
Emunos ve-Deos, 16
England, 23, 32, 43, 47
Enlightenment of the Eyes, 25
Essence of Judaism, 58
Essenes, 11
Esther, Book of, 76
Ethical Monotheism, 6, 51
Exile, 8
Ezra, 9

F

Feisal, Emir, 43

Felsenthal, Bernard, 40
Ferdinand, King, 21
Flavius, Clemens, 103
France, French, 33, 41, 43, 47
Frank, Jacob, 25
Fraternities, 100
Frederick William, 30
Freehof, Solomon B., 51, 86, 105, 107
French Revolution, 33
Fulvia, 103

G

Gaon, 15
Gaon of Vilna, 28
Gemarah, 13
Ger—stranger, convert, 102, 103
German, Germany, 26, 30, 31, 32, 34, 42, 45
Ghetto, 27
God, idea of, 51
Good and Evil, 61 ff
Golden Age, 18, 19
Graetz, Heinrich, 14, 103, 104
Great Britain, 47
Greek, Greek Culture, 10

H

Haganah, 46
Hasdai ibn Shaprut, 18
Hasmoneans, 10, 11
Hellenism, 10
Hebrew Union College, 40
Hebrew Union College—Jewish Institute of Religion, 97
Hebrew words and terms—see vocabulary, pages 108-112
Helen of Adiabne, 103
Herzl, Theodor, 41, 42
Hess, Moses, 42
Hezekiah, King, 5
Hias, United Service For Aid to Immigrants, 99
Hillel Foundation, 100
Hirsch, Samuel, 40
History of the Jews, Graetz, 103, 104
Hitler, Adolph, 42, 45, 101
Holidays, Jewish, 70 ff
Holland, 22, 31
Home, the Jewish, 69 ff
Homilies, of The Jews, Historically Developed, The, 35

Hope of Israel, The, 31
Hoveve Zion, 42

I

Immortality, 64, 73
Inquisition, 20, 21, 36
Intermarriage, 83
Isaac, 1
Isaiah, 24, 54
Israel, 4, 6
Israel Baal Shem Tove (Besht)
    Master of the Good Name, 27
Israel ben Eliezer (Besht), 27
Islam, 14
Israel, people of, 6, 54 ff
Israel—The Jewish State, 46, 47, 48,
    99
Italy, 47
Izates, 103

J

Javneh, Javnia, 13
Jacob, 1, 2
Jacobson, Israel, 34
Jehuda ha-Levi, 18
Jehudah ha-Nasi, 13
Jeremiah, 6
Jewish Homeland, 43, 46
Jewish Community Center, 98
Jewish Labor Committee, 99
Jewish National Home, 99
Jewish Publication Society, 99
Jewish Welfare Board, 98
Jewish Welfare Fund, 98
Job, 61, 62
Jochanan ben Zakkai, 13
Joint Distribution Committee,
    American Jewish, 47
Joseph Ha Cohen, 25
Josiah, King, 6, 7
Judah Maccabeus, 10
Judah Messer Leon, 25
Judaism, Basic Concepts of, 50, 51 ff
—, Definition of, 51, 56
Judenstaat, A Jewish State, 41
Judah, Judea, 4, 5, 9, 10, 11
Judah ben Gerim, 103
Judaism, 14
Judaism, Conversion to, 105 ff
Judaism, study of, 106
Justice, 51, 58

K

Kaddish prayer, 65
Kallah—institute for study, 13
Karaism, Karaites, 16
Khazars, 17
Kiddush, sanctification, 70, 81, 89
Kohler, Kaufman, 57
Kol Nidre, 73

L

Ladino, 22
Lancaster, Pennsylvania, 37
Lessing, Gotthold Ephraim, 32, 33
Levi, Leo N. Memorial Hospital,
    Hot Springs, 99
Liberal, Liberals, Liberalism, 36, 38,
    40
Life and Death 63 ff
Lilienthal, Max, 40
Lithuania, 25
Los Angeles, 105
Luria, Isaac, 24
Luther, Martin, 29, 30

M

Maccabeans, 10
Machuza, 13
Maimonides, Moses, 18, 19
Man, Concept of, 52 ff
Manasseh ben Israel, 31, 32
Marrano, 21, 36
Marriage, 83 ff
Massoretes, 16
Mater Synagogarum, 103
May Laws, 41
Meir of Rothenberg, 20
Memorial Service, 73, 86
Missionaries, 102
Monabaz, 103
Mendelssohn, Moses, 32, 33
Messiah, 12, 24, 31
Messiahs, false, 25
Messianic era, 63
Mexico, 36
Micah, 6
Middle East, 5, 44
Mishnah, 13, 103
Mishneh Torah, 19
Misnagdim, 29

Mohammed, Mohammedanism, 15, 104
Molcho, David, 25
Moral law, 55, 56
Moral purpose, 54
Moreh Nebuchim—Guide to the Perplexed, 19
Moses, 4
Moslem empire, 15
Mourning, 85
Music, 69

N

National Socialism, 42
Napoleon, 33
Nebuchadnezzar, 7
Nehardea, 13
New Amsterdam, 37
Newport, Rhode Island, 37
New Year, 71 ff
New York, 37, 105
New York Federation of Reform Synagogues, 97, 105

O

Oliphant, Laurence, 42
Onkelos, 103
Orthodox, orthodoxy, 25, 40, 48, 80, 84, 106

P

Palestine, 2, 42, 43, 44, 45, 46, 47, 66
Patriarchs, 1, 2
Peru, 36
Pesach, 76 ff
Pharisees, 11
Philadelphia, 105
Piyyutim, 28
Poland, 25, 26, 29, 40, 44, 45
Popes, 25
Portugal, Portuguese, 21, 31, 36
Posnanski, M. Gustav, 39
Potocki, Valentin Count, 104
Prayer, 59 ff
Prophets, 7
Proselytes, 21
Proselytism in the Talmudic Period, 103
Protestant Reformation, 29, 30

Psalms, psalmist, 59, 60
Ptolemies, 10
Pumbeditha, 13, 15
Purim—Feast of Lots, 76

R

Rabbi, 67, 96, 105
Reading List, 113, 114
Reform, Reform Judaism, 33, 34, 35, 42, 78, 106
Reform Judaism in America, 39, 48
Reform Jewish Practice, 51, 86, 107
Religious school, 82, 83
Repentance, 53, 72
Resurrection of the dead, 57
Reubeni, David, 25
Revolutionary War, 101
Richard the Lion-hearted, 23
Righteousness, 5, 51
Rome, 11, 12, 14, 103
Rothschild, Baron Edmund de, 42
Rudolph of Hapsburg, 20
Rumania, 40
Russia, Russian, 25, 26, 29, 40, 41, 42, 44
Ruth—Book of, 102

S

Saadia Gaon, 61
Sabbath, 70 ff
Sabbathai Zeir, 25
Sadducees, 11
Safed, 24
Salvation, 57 ff
Samaria, 4
Samaritans, 9
Samuel, Sir Herbert, 43
Sanhedrin, 33
Savannah, Georgia, 37
Saul, King, 2, 3
Saul of Tarsus, 12
Scholastics, 19
Scriptures, 9, 11, 16, 30, 35, 55, 67
Seder service, 70, 76, 77
Seleucid Kings, 10
Sephardic, 22, 112
Sermon, 67
Shovuos—Feast of Weeks, 77 ff
Shulchan Aruch—Prepared Table, 25
Separation of Church and State, 38

Sforno, Obadiah, 25
Shemah, 6, 70, 84
Shtadlan, 26
Simon ben Yohai, 23
Silver, Abba Hillel, 62, 64
Sin, 53
Sinai Congregation, Chicago, 39
Smolenskin, Perez, 42
Social responsibility, 57 ff
Soferim, 9
Solomon ibn Gabirol, 18
Solomon, Haym, 101
Solomon, King, 3, 4
Sororities, 100
South Africa, 48
South America, 48
Spain, 15, 17, 18, 19, 20, 21, 22
Spinoza, 31
Suffering, 62
Stuyvesant, Peter, 36
Sukkah, 74
Sukkos—Feast of Tabernacles, 74 ff
Sura, 13, 15, 17
Synagogue, 8, 13, 14, 35, 38, 45, 48, 56, 60, 66 ff, 96 ff, 100, 105, 106
Synagogue organizations, 96 ff

T

Talmud, 14, 16, 20, 23, 55
Tannaim, interpreters of the law, 13
Temple (at Jerusalem), 3, 66
Temple, Temples, 35, 68
Ten Commandments, 7, 53, 71
Ten Tribes, 5
Teshuvah, repentance, 53, 72
Theocracy, 9
Theology, 51, 58
Thirteen Principles, 19
Thirty Years' War, 30
Titus, 12
Torah, 9, 11, 13, 22, 27, 56 ff, 75
Truman, Harry S., 47
Turkey, 22, 25
Tze-enah u-Re-enah, 26

U

Union of American Hebrew Congregations, 40, 97 ff, 105
Union Prayerbook, Union Home Prayerbook, 73, 86 ff

United Jewish Appeal, 99
United Nations, 46
United States, 43, 47, 96
United States, Jewish population in the Eighteenth C., 38, 39
—, Jewish population in the Twentieth C., 48, 96
United Synagogue of America, 97
Unity of Mankind, 52, 55
Uriel da Costa, 31
United Palestine Appeal, 47

V

Vaad Arba Aratzoth—Council of Four Lands, 25
Vale of Tears, 25
Versailles Peace Conference, 43
Vespasian, 12
Vilna, 28
Visigoth rulers of Spain, 18

W

Washington, George, 37
Wessely, Naphtali Hertz, 32
Where Judaism Differed, 62, 64
William the Conqueror, 23
Wise, Isaac Mayer, 40
Wise, Stephen S., 43
Wissenschaft des Judentums, 35
World War I, 43, 44
World War II, 44, 45, 47
Worship, 59 ff

Y

Yahveh, 2, 3
Yiddish, 26

Z

Zaddik, Zaddikim, 28
Zalman, Shneor, 29
Zealots, 12
Zion, 44, 48, 56
Zionism, 41, 42
Zionist Congress, 42
Zionist Movement, 42
Zionist Organization of America, 99
Zohar, 23
Zunz, Leopold, 35